ROMANIA UNDER THE TYRANNY OF SMALL FIGURES

BY

Ilie Şerbănescu

Translated from the Romanian by Adriana Cerkez

EAST EUROPEAN MONOGRAPHS, BOULDER, CO
DISTRIBUTED BY COLUMBIA UNIVERSITY PRESS, NEW YORK

2007

East European Monographs, No. DCCV

ISBN: 978-0-88033-603-1
Library of Congress Control Number: 2007927319

Printed in the United States of America

I am grateful to:

My wife Marina for her irreplaceable support in conceiving, structuring, and editing the present book;

Mr. Daniel Daianu who kept supporting me in writing a different kind of economic and political book

Miss Bianca Stancu and Miss Monica Mihailescu for the careful final “translation” of a negligent manuscript.

TABLE OF CONTENTS

PART II

THE MAIN PROBLEMS IN ECONOMY: APPROACHES AND RESULTS

List of abbreviations

APMPS – Authority for Privatization and Management of State Participations

ASU – Agricultural State Unit

AVBA – Agency for Valuing Bank Assets

CEC – The Central Savings Bank (of Romania)

CEFTA – Central European Free Trade Area

COMECOM – Council for Mutual Economic Assistance

DP – Democratic Party

DUMR – Democratic Union of the Magyars in Romania

EBRD – European Bank for Reconstruction and Development

FIS – Financial Investment Society

GDP – Gross Domestic Product

GRP – Great Romania Party

IMF – International Monetary Fund

NAIER – The National Association of Importers and Exporters in Romania

NCM – National Commission of Movables

NIF – National Investment Fund

NLP – National Liberal Party

NPP – National Peasant Party (Christian Democratic)

NSF – National Salvation Front

PPF – Private Property Fund

PSDR – Party of Social Democracy in Romania

RBD – Romanian Bank for Development

RBFT – Romanian Bank for Foreign Trade

RCB – Romanian Commercial Bank

RDC – Romanian Democratic Convention

RENEL – National Autonomous (State) Company for Electric Power Distribution

RSI – Romanian Intelligence Service

SMO – Small and Medium Organization

SPF – State Property Fund

INTRODUCTION

Common people, obliged as they are to judge things quite concretely, cannot help gawping at the storm an agreement with IMF provokes in the government each time when such amounts as $70–100 millions are involved. They know less about conditionality, lending rates, green light for external financing, etc. but they are sensitive to what they hear: that money finally enters Romania. However, they know pretty well that $70–100 million is the amount a self-respecting club can afford to pay for two famous football players.

Making a fuss over $70–100 million is both ridiculous and embarrassing. Unfortunately, the disgraceful character of such an amount perfectly expresses the tragic-comical situation reached by the thin and impoverished Romanian economy that hardly gets on under the fiercest of all tyrannies: that of small figures.

Almost everything in the Romanian economy is measured in small figures. The only exceptions seem to be inflation, with two-figure yearly rates, and thefts, which are simply huge.

The monthly average wage in Romania is about $100 and it is more and more difficult to keep it at that level; about 9–10 million Romanians live on less than $1/day: the so-called "eastern" limit of poverty.

The international rating agencies penalized the Romanian failure and thus emphasized the small figures that tyrannically dominate, in a vicious circle, Romanian economy. They even proclaimed, more often than not gratuitously, that Romania would default on external payments. Likewise, the solution of introducing a Monetary Council in Romania was insistently peddled although such a thing would have not been possible in Romania with its only $2–3 billion currency reserves. Those who want a Monetary Council in Romania will have to put at its disposal about $10 billion. Otherwise, the national currency will drop, prices will skyrocket, and the average wage will reduce to $25–30 as happened in Bulgaria. However, the tendency to smaller and smaller figures in the Romanian economy will remain.

In 1999, in the absence of a normal access to external resources, Romania was forced to experiment an external adjustment assessed at about $1.6 billion. According to the present international standards the amount is insignificant but it meant the reduction of each working person's average income by about 4 wages of the 12 monthly wages. However if the real wage dropped to $30/month in case of collapse an external adjustment similar to the one in 1999 would be equivalent to the whole amount paid for wages in Romania!

Romania's yearly domestic saving is expressed in embarrassing figures: $3.5–4 billion or about 10–12% GDP equivalent in comparison with 20–30% in a normal country. It is this small amount that the budget, banks, insurance companies, and investments funds hustle about. Therefore there is no wonder that the interests are extremely high sometimes. The bulk of money is directly or indirectly taken by the State for financing the budgetary deficit: directly by public issues and indirectly by government securities bought by the commercial banks after they had attracted deposits from the population and from the economic organizations. Since these investments are safe (at least for the time being) there is no money left on the market for real economy. Without financing, real economy stagnates. A vicious circle that can only generate even smaller figures!

The smaller and smaller figures are also favored by small investments: the desperate attempt to protect somehow the population's consumption in a stagnant or quasi-stagnant economy at the expense of reducing investments subverted Romania's development chance. With investments representing only 17–18% GDP equivalent, Romania is like a truck having a runabout engine. With annual investments of $5–6 billion, the equivalent amount an informatics company invests in research-development only, Romania cannot afford the slightest economic development that could release it from the tyranny of small figures.

Unfortunately, the budget cannot contribute significantly. With tax collections and social contributions of only $10 billion Romania is unable to solve the economic and social problems facing it.

Instead of being idled, people were pensioned off before age. In this way, a rather strange situation has been reached: 4.4 million working people have to support more than 6.2 million pensioners. Therefore, the State budget has to support the bankrupt national insurance budget. Besides the pension scheme, the $6-billion State budget has other "duties" as well: to support the bankrupt industrial organizations and the so-called "bank restructuring", in fact non-performing loans with no chance of being ever returned. Mention should be made that a $6-billion State budget is the budget of one of the smallest Swiss cantons with several hundreds of thousands inhabitants only.

In fact, the tyranny of small figures starts from the Romanian economy productive capacity quantified by the Gross Domestic Product: about $35 billion, representing the equivalent of the annual sales of an average western transnational company. However, the productive capacity is best illustrated by exports that represent the competitive ability of the domestic production on foreign markets. For several years the Romanian exports kept vegetating around $8–8.5 billion. In 2000, pushed up by the *leu* devaluation and by privileged taxation of the profits got from foreign deliveries, they succeeded to be higher than $10 billion a proof that their limits reside in the production structure. Trapped as they are in the same production structure for about 20–30 years, the exports have remained the same for 20–30 years (wood, metals, raw minerals, ready-made clothes, and footwear) with no chance whatever to develop and to save economy from the tyranny of small figures. The Romanian exports are the smallest/inhabitant in Europe: 22 million Romanian hardly succeed to export the equivalent of the exports made by 9 million Hungarians or 700 000 Dutchmen.

The Gross Domestic Product shows execrable labor productivity and a completely inefficient resource allocation; it is sometimes equal to the turnover of a private western company having 200–250 thousand employees.

Romania can develop provided that it is helped by direct foreign investments. However, structural changes can only be made if these investments exceed a "critical mass" of about $10–12 billion, i.e. at least $5–7 billion above the present level. It is a trifle for the present international standards – a small figure indeed. However, it is huge for Romania which lives under the tyranny of small figures!

PART I

ROMANIAN TRANSITION: AN EXPENSIVE IMPROVISATION

CHAPTER 1

Coordinates of an economic failure

More than a decade has elapsed since the dramatic events of December 1989. Leaving their cause aside – a coup or a popular revolution – they have opened a new page in the history of Romania and that is for sure: passing from communism to capitalism, from totalitarianism to democracy, from command economy to market economy.

Economically speaking, the period is a failure. Out of the eleven years between 1990 and 2000, six recorded a strong economic decrease and the other five a poor economic development that is still a debatable topic: has it meant a real progress or quite the opposite? The first three years of decrease were equally imputed: to the objective effects generated by the destruction of the old structures and by the disappearance of the old markets that had been politically ensured by COMECOM; to improper populism; delay in starting reform; and to the erratic policy of the first Iliescu-Roman governments.

In the following four years – those of Văcăroiu government – the economic decline stopped and the level of the Gross Domestic Product started recovering. However, Văcăroiu economic recovery is still extremely controversial since it was achieved by stimulating industrial activity before restructuring it, an action considered detrimental to the extent that costs exceeded benefits. Even more, it was practically financed by unbalancing Romania's domestic accounts and by forcing the external ones.

The payment reached its term after1996 and had to be paid then, irrespective of the governing party. That meant a deterioration of the living standard both directly through the reduction of social spending and indirectly through inflation and national currency devaluation. Unfortunately, the 1996–2000 administration accepted the IMF program as such, with no adaptation whatever. They tried to replace the structure reforms – that had not been practically attacked until 1997, but could only be achieved gradually and in a longer time, maybe years – with a series of macroeconomic measures regarding foreign currency and customs liberalization along with monetary and budgetary restrictions. All this had to be applied in a few weeks and confused the entire economy unprepared to take over all the shocks at the same time. Therefore, the economic fall was unavoidable and the cost paid for the balance of the domestic budget and for part of the external debts was even more difficult to bear.

However, the $ 19 billion external debts made during 11years just to get a dramatic GDP decrease and an even more dramatic one in the buying power must have been a unique performance, if not simple economic crap. At least, the remaining debt (about half) enabled a slower decrease in the living standard than that imposed by the mentioned economic counter-performance.

After 11 years of transition, the Romanian economy is disastrous. In 2000, GDP represented only 76% of the GDP in 1989. However, that decrease was only partly due to the beneficial giving up of the "ballast" of production for production's sake; the rest was caused by the reduction of economic activity caused by a dramatic fall in investments. Before 1989, the investments in GDP used to represent more than 30% yearly and they even reached 30–40% sometimes. In 2000, they were 17–18%. In 10–11 years just a few factories for bottling beer and soft drinks added to the industrial map of Romania. It is hard or rather impossible to get economic growth under such circumstances.

Giving up ballast does not solve the problem, it just makes the boat lighter, easier to row, and the wreck risk is less.

Without a good engine to replace the ballast the boat will drift and will never be able to reach a safe destination.

Public consumption could only follow a descending line as well. Although it absorbs more than 70% of GDP, compared to 50–55% before 1989, it is generally lower because 70% of a lower GDP (76%) represents, in absolute terms, less!

More serious is the fact that without investments to replace the deserted production (because it is not competitive or it has no markets) deindustrialization rather than restructuring occurs. The process – tragic and real as it is – that PSDR ascribed to the governments following 1996 started in fact during Iliescu administrations. Political and ideological reasons made those administrations keep the entire industrial spectrum, without restructuring it, although it was obvious that Romania would have never the required resources to save its entire industry. The only sensible solution would have been therefore to leave a part of it aside and to save the rest. In the attempt to save the whole industry with useless resource injections, Iliescu administrations compromised it entirely. If, in 1989, certain sectors and activities in Romania had some competitive advantage at the world level, it has been lost, since all the industrial branches in Romania are out of date and lack the adequate resources to revamp.

The 1996–2000 administration had to take over that deindustrialization process and emphasized it by applying the IMF programs of macro-stabilization and restructuring without money. However, mention should be made that the respective process would have advanced no matter how, irrespective of the governing party (or parties) and of the program implemented since a vicious circle had already been created. The more numerous companies became useless and superannuated because of their lack of competitiveness the less the ability to mobilize resources to replace them was. Romania has already reached that stage when it lacks even the required money to close down unproductive companies, not to say a word about putting something else instead. What we could have done several years ago, when there was still some beef, it is impossible to do now when all the beef has been eaten up. Without an investment impulse from abroad a normal start cannot be made.

In 11 years Romania lost, in formal economy, about 3.5–3.6 million workplaces, most of them in industry. One million people are unemployed and 2.6 million retired (most of them before age). The absurd situation has been reached (economically, impossible to overpass) when there exist more pensioners, i.e. beneficiaries of the State pension scheme, than working people contributing to that pension scheme. Without significant investments, the tendency of economic dilution could no longer be stopped and it struck like a bulldozer. The half restructuring did not work and consequently Romania could not get an increase of efficiency in the real sector of economy, but a production decrease only.

Overwhelmed by tasks it has no connection with – support of bankrupt economic organizations, survival of pension scheme, improvement of banking system – the public budget cannot practically produce important amounts of money to help development. As privatization has not been implemented in due time, it can no longer be a restructuring and investment solution since each asset unit is loaded with at least two debt units. Therefore, the chance to sell loads and not business is a poor one indeed; it is even zero in most of the cases. Now, when 11 years have elapsed from the so-called passing to a market economy, its basis, i.e. private property, is still in the minority. Industry is simply overwhelmed by the State propriety which survives in monopolies that keep at a distance any competitive prospect. About half of the State property, organized in the so-called autonomous (State) companies (a kind of monopolies), was kept far from the influence of privatization and on a long term that proved to be a disastrous decision that compromised any chance of restructuring in this sector. Out of the other half of State property, organized in the co-called trading companies, only two-fifths have been privatized and, according to the official statistics, more than a third has no chance of being privatized.

Under such circumstances, the poor performances of the Romanian economy should wonder nobody. As its basis has remained unchanged, the Romanian economy is characterized today, as it was before 1989, by the same lack of efficiency and of competitiveness. The only difference is that one of the two safety valves permitting inefficiency and lack of competitiveness emerge – that of prices – has been opened. The other safety valve – unemployment that represents the very expression and consequence of restructuring – has been kept shut for all the mentioned period. Since unemployment has not been accepted as a correction lever in economy, the entire lack of competitiveness is reflected in prices that have thus no chance of getting lower. In fact, the Romanian economy has moved on with no change at all, year after year, to a higher and higher price landing.

Whereas economy has practically stayed the same, the half-decentralization and the half-introduction of some market mechanisms resulted in somehow different consequences of the equally poor economic performances. Huge price hikes have replaced lack of products: before there was no meat, now there is no money to buy it! Social disparities have replaced the relative uniformity of poverty without inducing motivation for working since disparities have rather extra economic causes: monopolistic positions of several State enterprises and, even more serious, thefts, tax evasion, speculation, corruption and other crimes. National welfare has been redistributed: very few people receive a disproportionately large share while the huge majority of them receive disproportionately little.

Therefore, most of the people cannot be satisfied by the transition offers at material and economic levels, respectively. For this majority, the genuinely great achievements of the new epoch – freedom of expression and freedom to travel – have already lost their meaning. They can now openly express their protest against losing their jobs and against the dramatic fall in the buying power of their incomes but they might prefer their jobs and the stable prices before instead. In fact they were able to murmur their dissatisfaction during communism, as well! There are about 17 million adults in Romania entitled to have passports but only about four million have them. Out of the latter, about one million only tries to benefit from their right to travel – because of financial reasons – but they have to face the "wall" built by the western countries in their attempt to protect themselves against the poor, trespassers, and criminals.

There are some people who would like to see the old times revive, but Romania can no longer go back. Even if it wanted it had no place to. Time has changed. Capitalism is everywhere around us and everywhere in the world. A ruthless capitalism that one has to adapt to, or to disappear. All that matters is to be among winners and not among losers. And that means to be competitive above all. Otherwise one cannot resist in the ruthless international competition that can throw you out of your own markets.

At least up to now Romania has been an economic failure of transition, maybe one of the most revealing in the ex-communist area. We cannot find a better explanation since the lives of so many Romanians have changed for the worse. Based on criteria used for all the other ex-communist countries, the World Bank appreciates that the poor in Romania represent two fifths of the whole population. This figure has systematically increased year after year although the population has decreased as a result of emigration and of the dramatic fall in birth rate. These poor people of Romania cannot see something that does not exist – the transition success – but only facts: misfortune, lack of security in the street, atrophy of the State authority in spite of the institutions proliferation, shameless theft, and ostentatious opulence that oppress and disgust them. Too much poverty and too much theft overwhelm the balance of the Romanian transition.

CHAPTER 2

The reform – nothing but efficacy

After so many years of reform "hide and seek", the things are practically so complicated that nobody knows exactly where to start from to break the logjam. The constraints used to get the so-called economic macro-stabilization have been pushed too far and about half of the Romanians are poor. Even more alarming is the fact that these constraints have drained the resources the economy needed for restructuring. Romania has not the necessary money for "demolition" (otherwise, necessary) to say nothing of construction instead. Thus we have to face a circular problem between nonproductive macro-stabilization and hypothetical restructuring.

Macro-stabilization is the reform at the surface of the economy. Restructuring is its very essence and represents reform at a macroeconomic level, at the level of the enterprises, the basis of economy.

Macro-stabilization focuses on an important reduction of inflation and on the relative stabilization of exchange rate by equilibrating the giant economic aggregates: market demand and offer, population's consumption and incomes, money supply, credit, budget (State incomes and expenditures), Romania's external accounts.

Nevertheless, the essence of reform is restructuring since reform is achieved through it. It is neither high philosophy nor a bogey to worry about for a country in transition; it is simply a most natural and necessary process of resources reallocation from inefficient activities towards efficient ones.

The resources (energy, material, financial, people) engaged in unproductive or without market activities are wasted instead of being used in potentially productive and with market activities. This waste compromises the efforts made to turn other activities competitive, reduces the general level of economic efficiency and diminishes the incomes and the living standard of the population. Without essential changes in the real sector of economy, that should lead to an efficient reallocation of resources, any movement of resources at the economy surface, in search for the so-called macroeconomic stabilization, remains a simple pawn movement with no importance whatsoever on a chess board on which the heavy, decisive pieces are not moved at all.

This has been the state of things in the Romanian economy for over a decade. The resources, few as they were, were moved to and fro at the surface of economy in an attempt to find a balance that could not be reached without restructuring towards efficiency the real sector at the basis of economy. The loss-generating enterprises have remained unchanged and the unproductive activities have gone on. Thus, the attempts to find balance at a macroeconomic level are even more difficult and unsuccessful, while the relative balance, reached sometimes, is fragile, precarious, and transient.

Romanian transition is an economic and social failure because of three main reasons: a difficult communist inheritance; the absence of change strategy standing for lack of will; political, economic, and geographic position of Romania outside the sphere of the western interest.

Romanian economy in general, and mainly industry, are the result of the most orthodox communism in the south-eastern Europe, where resource allocation was made almost exclusively following political criteria, arbitrarily and voluntarily obeying commands and orders of the party, while holding the market signals in contempt. From this point of view, passing to market economy was extremely difficult, maybe the most difficult in all the countries of the region.

In 1989, the system crisis of communism in Romania had already started to manifest itself in what communism declared to be fundamental, i.e. production. An important downturn in production, the industrial one included, already existed at the end of the 1980s and another one, even more dramatic, was thought to be unavoidable in the years to come. The Romanian industrial model, concentrated on economically declining industries, could not have followed another direction. All kind of dearth had already appeared, a sign that crisis was almost imminent, although the State machinery put down the two main safety valves – inflation and unemployment. Romania was to enter the last decade of the 20th century with an enormous economic gap between demand and offer expressed by the fact that the money availability in the market had but one seventh cover in goods and services. The inflation potential was therefore devastating.

If such an inheritance – that is not an excuse but a reality – adds to the reform substitute characterizing the economic policy in Romania following December 1989, meaning in essence half measures in the reform at a macroeconomic level and practically no reform at all at a microeconomic one, leaving aside the fact that the institutional reform was zero, we can easily understand why Romania has reached the vicious circle it is struggling today in.

It was an embarrassing political and poor economic show to watch a country worshiping an idol: the present Romanian industrial model. The most confusing homage paid as far back as 1990 to that idol was the improper populism in favor of the industrial working class through direct conversion of the old investment allocations in wage raises that almost doubled the existing disequilibrium confronting the Romanian economy. One year following the events in December 1989, when the fist frail measures for a market economy had been initiated, the cover in goods of the money availability decreased to less than one tenth, making the reform even more difficult. Since the reform was placed under the sign of saving the industrial model by all means, in spite of it being a failure, and as a lot of ideological and political hesitations existed in passing to a market economy, the Romanian transition turned into an extremely expensive improvisation, economically and socially alike.

A lot of researchers and analysts try to define the post-December economic improvisation in Romania: it obviously can be called neither "shock therapy" nor "gradualism". The most suitable characterization seems to be "pathological gradualism" because it suggestively expresses the unhealthy significance of the half measures that can only lead to a dead point, leaving no perspective at all.

The half measures in the economic reform promoted under the sign of social tolerability doubled in fact their social costs. Even graver, these half measures created a kind of vicious circle, as they perpetuated themselves in time and failed to reach, even gradually, the goals they had been meant to. And it was not quite accidental that the economic reform in Romania showed only the pains it inevitably was to produce and not the economic performances it was supposed to generate.

As understanding as one can be in describing the post-December experience, one cannot help noticing the almost complete lack of pinning down the economic and social goals. In this crucial situation for a country, the things were too much influenced by the ideological doubts of the president ruling the country in the first seven years of this interval. For so many years he systematically avoided to state openly his opinion in favor of market economy, as he knew that it represented the capitalism lavishly criticized before and not the socialism in praise in the old days. That is the reason why Romania had no clear goal to follow; it did not know where it was going to, or what kind of transition it was experiencing. It is no wonder then that we reached nowhere.

Market economy was not even included in the initial program of those that took over the power in Romania in December 1989 and ruled in the crucial period at the beginning. As a desideratum, the idea of market economy appeared much later and rather vaguely, with no clear objectives; it was rather a catch phrase launched under the pressure of events, of the general trend around, just to receive some external financing. It was absolutely clear that the post-December power had no initial intention to implement market economy.

It is really upsetting that the target-goals were not been made clearer in time. When, due to the very improvisation in economy, the social polarization lost control, the administration finally formulated a goal, the insidious goal of "social market economy". The government must have felt that it would be embarrassing to convey on the impression that, under such circumstances, Romania could make for an equitable society and they tried, using that collocation, to avoid being made responsible for deepening the social gap. Nevertheless "social market economy" sounded rather awkward as social polarization gradually appeared to be the only tangible achievement of the Romanian transition. On the other side, Romania neither proved to be a market economy nor did it seem to move into that direction. At the same time, it is rather astonishing that not even after expressing its option to integrate into the European Union and after getting the association with the Western European organization (that represented a genuine earthquake for the Romanian economy), the way to market economy was not structured in clear objectives, to say nothing of a strategy for removing the bankrupt industrial model that suffocated the creation of an economy based on such criteria as efficiency and profitability. A strategy appeared only in 2000 and only as a result of the European Union pressures following the invitation made to Romania to take part in integration negotiations at some time in the future.

It is undeniable that Romania is situated outside western economic and political interests with whatever that implies. The only controversy lies in reasons and explanations.

CHAPTER 3

Why does not reform work!

The economic stiffness along with social polarity, in other words, lack of reform, has strictly political reasons. Probably the most important problem existing in the political sphere influencing the reform could be formulated as: the contradiction between the *reallocation* of resources implied by reform and *distribution* of resources the political forces make for their own sake. The bulk of facts gathered in the administrations before 1996 and after that clearly show that the parties expect to economically strengthen their political present and future once they have acceded to the power. They are thus subject to a double pressure: from their own members, who want economic, or rather material advantages, since they support the cause; and from their "sponsors" who have their strong reasons to support the party. The probably willful lack of clear legal provisions stipulating the financing of the political parties played a negative role in that direction.

Passing from a system of economic organization based on everybody's property, in fact of no one's, to one based on private property implies an unavoidable process of distributing the wealth of nation. These distributions of agricultural and industrial assets, of the control on the national wealth at as small as possible prices, even as a political gift, represent the main priority of the parties in either side of the political spectrum. The problem is that this process – finally unavoidable – regarded by the political parties as their main priority takes place when the reform has become economy's main priority. This represents, in fact, the change of the present structures and ways of counterproductive allocation of resources, and proves to be highly inefficient and can only generate domestic poverty and lack of competitiveness abroad.

As a matter of fact an economy similar to the present Romanian one can offer nothing else as it allocates energy, raw materials, and wage funds for products sold at lower prices or not sold at all, and systematically increases taxes for those paying them so that the budget can survive despite those who cook the books to avoid paying taxes. One can easily notice the contradiction between an efficient reallocation of products, implied by reform, and the interest of the political parties to distribute the resources among their political clientele or to get control over them. The effect is nefarious: while the reallocation of resources is delayed, the resources divided among the political forces or distributed on a cliental basis do not get a social function, through investments, and thus the wastes in varied forms of immediate consumption (mansions, expensive cars, journeys abroad, money for parties, politically interested sponsorships) become more important.

In order to hide these departures from the social function of resources, a false and detrimental social security replaces the necessary measures, unpopular of course, for efficient reallocation of resources.

It is obvious that those distributing resources to their own advantage cannot ask for sacrifices from the population; instead, they indirectly impose those sacrifices. This can explain the hypocritical crowd in the social-democratic area of the political spectrum, so often used as a demagogical hedge to protect obscure interests and savage capitalism. Under these conditions, the resources diminish: what is to be distributed is getting less and less while the process of creating new ones is markedly and dangerously slowing down. In this way, reform has fewer and fewer chances to come out of the vicious circle it has gone into.

Another problem in the political space, linked to the previous one, is constitutional. There exists an institutional deficit in Romania. When something starts it seldom comes to an end because of the institutions that are not in a position to deal with that issue or are not able to manage it. More than that, all kinds of obstacles dictated by cliental interests are created.

Public administration and the government itself are defectively conceived and organized, highly bureaucratic and consequently inefficient. Broadly speaking, their present organization repeats the communist one and has no connection with the institutional demands for promoting reform. For instance, each ministry in the Romanian government manages – we do not comment if it is good or bad – the "slice" of the official economy in its "parish" instead of conceiving, developing, and monitoring policies for the State and private sectors it is responsible for. Therefore, with the only exception of the Ministry of Finance, that rules the roost and has to put its seal of approval on almost every normative act, all the other government entities (ministry or agency) with an integrating or synthesis role are unheeded.

However, the number of government's agencies increased instead of being reduced. Likewise, they are overstaffed. This is strictly dictated by cliental interests and that phenomenon is even more extravagant when a coalition of parties accedes to administration. The algorithm – that is the power-sharing of the positions in the public administration among the parties of the coalition – has thus become a kind of coalition excrescence meant to satisfy the varied and sometimes opposite pressures coming from the political forces supporting the government in the Parliament. Governmental agencies were created to find a place for the representatives of one political force or another and even worse to counterbalance or compromise, by diluting the act of decision making, another structure belonging, according to the algorithm, to another political force in the coalition. Although since the end of 2000 there has been only one ruling party, the long-expected "compress" of the public administration has not taken place.

The number of the governmental agencies could be reduced to less than one third, and that of the staff working in public administration to less than a half with no problem at all. On the contrary, the effect will be beneficial to the budget. If the economic reform is not accompanied, or better preceded, by an institutional one, starting with the very government of Romania, the former will be never implemented.

CHAPTER 4

When the game rules are absent

The fact that the reform does not work in Romania and, consequently, the performance in the Romanian economy is far from good is almost purely political but it is not only the result of the institutional deficit and of the pork-barrel politics. Twelve years have elapsed since the events in 1989 and practically none of the basic rules of the market economy has been established by the main actors on the Romanian political, economic, and social scene: neither those regulating the property, the role of the State in economy (not even broadly), the relations between politicians and businesspeople, the relations between State and the business background, those between State and small and medium business in particular, nor those relating to the position towards domestic and foreign capitals, respectively. Everything is shrouded in a counterproductive mist, the regulations are unstable and in permanent change according to circumstances and to the colors of the political parties although a general thread should exist in these fields. The short historical time cannot be a permanent excuse. More than that, the alternation of the governing parties occurred in 1996, later than in other countries in transition, and in 2000 a complete political cycle was closed when the losers in the previous elections acceded to power again.

4.1. Property – an issue to be solved

Not even now, when more than 12 years have elapsed since the events in December 1989, the issue of property has been solved yet. However, there are sectors where some solutions were found but they do not correspond to the Euro-Atlantic standards. It is not important here if these standards are good or bad, and if they can be adapted or not to Romania. Romania wants to belong to the Euro-Atlantic structures, so it has to quickly assimilate those standards, even if it dislikes them: the Euro-Atlantic world will never accept Romania to waive rules in the very matter of property, the basis of their value system.

For seven years, out of political reasons, the first Iliescu administrations practically refused to solve the property issue according to the western system of values. On the contrary, they adopted some regulations the effects of which stalled an adequate resolution. In fact, nobody expected a better thing!

However the biggest failure was recorded by the RDC-DP administration since almost all the forces in the coalition had committed themselves to solve this issue.

The failure has got precise causes: 1) Petre Roman's DP did not intend, more exactly they did not want to solve it. Quite the opposite, they sabotaged most of the solutions from the very beginning. Their approach was systematical, programmed, and professionally worked out so that Romania was put out of the running for Europe. Ironically, they seemed to be the most eager to see Romania in Europe. 2) Democratic Convention that had made of the property issue their electoral, ideological, and doctrinal banner was more interested in power and in their seats in ministries and in the Parliament than in finding a solution. So, they accepted all the blackmails and played in DP hands instead of breaking coalition as soon as they had realized what DP intentions were, since the latter revealed them almost from the very beginning. Let us admit that for the crucial issue of property, on which finally depended Romania's way to Europe, they should have run the risk of snap election. Instead, they preferred to keep their seats in ministries or in the Parliament.

I want to make it clear that NPP, the only party that had insisted on the property issue, had no excuse and they were in fact guilty for that failure. They loved so much their positions during the four years of the above-mentioned administration that they became completely oblivious of the century old and for centuries to come properties.

Constantinescu himself, the then president of Romania, was no better than the others. He should have shown more determination in making the things clear and should have not accepted DP's blackmail of breaking the coalition for the sake of keeping a chimera of stability, his slogan abroad in the name of an illusory hope that Romania would be admitted to join NATO. And an illusion it was!

The liberals – the NPP's colleagues in administration – had an ambiguous position although private property was the sacred basis of liberalism they were striving to make us believe they wanted to promote in Romania. The delay in promulgating a law on nationalized houses, ambiguity of some of its provisions, and mainly the purposely unclear way in which the Ministry of Justice (that was in Liberals' responsibility) worked out and promoted the Public Domain Law, that opened the way for all possible interpretations, turned the liberal attempt to change Constitution into a poor joke.

The NPP-NLP-DP coalition, with a majority in Parliament, did not succeed to adopt a new regulation regarding buildings and to replace the existing one inherited from the Iliescu regime. The inherited regulation accepted in principle a cosmetic retrocession, but practically limited it to the less frequent case when the legal owners (or their heirs) lived in that very building. It is common knowledge that nationalization or expropriation was purposely made to remove the owners from their houses. The coalition could have chosen another limitation, for instance retrocession in kind of one building or flat only and compensations for the rest of them in order to avoid the complex economic, political, and social problems generated by giving back the respective living spaces. More than that, the regulation gave the tenants inhabiting nationalized buildings the right to buy them, despite the fact that the legal owners had been identified and had claimed their houses back. It must be emphasized that such a regulation enacted in fact a theft. Ceausescu himself, who acted in the total despise of the private property, dared not do such a thing.

The bill of the then liberal minister of Justice to change those regulations tried to reconcile and left the problem of the living space completely ambiguous, although it was a matter of principle. And nothing should be left unclear when it comes to principles! In fact the liberals tried to soothe away the DP party and they did not seem to realize that the then DP leaders would never give up, in the name of retrocession principle, the comfortable houses they occupied in the Primaverii residential area.

In the last instance they tried to pass the law with the help of PSDR but they honorably gave up since PSDR, taking advantage of the situation, had introduced amendments that awarded compensations instead of retrocession in kind.

The property of the public administration is still foggy at central, county, and local levels, respectively. It is still not certain what belongs to the public sector and what to the State private domain and in each case at what level the delimitation problem has to be solved. For instance what is, in the built-in area, the town hall private property? What happens with the ground crossed by the mains? Who is responsible for the lakes within a locality? Who owns the ground under and around the high-tension poles? What kind of relation should exist between a town hall and those trying to use its buildings or lands? The

Puzdrea case, already famous, and those of the land exchange in which the Ministry of Defense is involved, are just consequences of the confusion existing in the Public Domain Law. All this confusion encourages abuses.

The law passed during the RDC-DP coalition did nothing to eliminate the confusion. Beyond the correct principle regulations, the law was rather vague when it came to concrete aspects. Its key is an annex supposed to itemize everything belonging to the Public Domain. The annex, taking advantage of the complexity of the cases, simply gives examples of solving the problem without offering concrete solutions. For the enforcement of law, the Ministry of Finance, that had to formulate the norms, asked the local authorities to itemize; the Ministry was then to establish the rules for delimiting the public domain. Everything stalled at this stage. Unfortunately the final regulation is the responsibility of the public administration at a central, county, or local level respectively and can be influenced by personal or group interests. The avoidance of the discretionary character will be the very key of a good law in Romania.

Likewise, it is hard to discuss about the tragedy characterizing the industrial property to be privatized. Following the laws passed in 1990 and 1991, the capital to be privatized in the State enterprises, re-called "trading companies", remained without an owner. The State gave up its managing position, a decision purposely rather than involuntarily confounded with relinquishing the owner's authority, and the situation generated serious dissolution and degradation that always occur where and when there is no owner.

It is no wonder then that the enterprises without an owner will always generate losses and arrears. If there is nobody's responsibility then you should be stupid not to generate losses and to pay your debts somehow. Although the RDC-DP administration changed the privatization laws several times, they never touched the crucial issue of the State enterprises to be privatized that had remained without owners. The only possible explanation is that the coalition political forces, similar to those before 1996, were not interested in clarifying the matter since they considered that those very ambiguities could be profitable.

Therefore the RDC-DP coalition left the situation of the properties in almost the same stage they had found it: a sensible law on the nationalized buildings was not passed; the law on giving back land was not enforced and it was to be changed by the future Parliament; the regulation delimiting the public domain was subject to discretion, pork-barrel politics, and corruption, while the industrial property to be privatized remained without an owner, another obstacle to privatization.

When PSDR came back following the elections of November 2000 the effect was the expected one. The coherence of one-party administration was obvious: some property problems were regulated – maybe as a result of the same old political, electoral, and cliental reasons – but several solutions adopted contradicted the western philosophy of property.

The new law was not what it pretended to be: a regulation concerning the restitution of the buildings forcibly seized by communists. Behind a lot of exceptions and conditions, the restoration in kind was replaced by potential compensations Therefore, in its present form, the buildings restoration law is a law of compensations.

The explanation is simple. The members of the Parliament preferred to award compensations because many of them or those close to them still live in nationalized houses and they do not intend to leave them to the benefit of the legal owners. These members of the Parliament belong to the whole political spectrum and as long as the population pays the compensations through the State budget they have nothing to lose.

Maybe the worst thing of all is that the law enacts the previous theft and considers buying of the nationalized houses as a fait accompli, according to the law passed by PSDR during its previous administration. There are so many members of the Parliament and their acolytes luxuriating in nationalized houses they bought almost for nothing although they knew exactly that such a transaction was against any norm regulating private property! Since the problem was solved through compensations, the Romanian political class, be it social-democratic or liberal, plays the generous role on account of public money, that is on somebody else's money. Therefore, young people in Romania, with no prospect and with low wages, forced to pay for something they have no business with, have one more reason to leave the country. The communist confiscations have to be assumed and all the restorations must be made in kind. On the other side, compensations, if the case might be, must be symbolical, purely symbolical because the innocents and the poor pay for them and not the guilty ones.

According to the changes in the law on giving back land – mainly the proof with papers (the witnesses are not accepted) for the 1945 situation – a lot of legal owners cannot receive their lands and forests as the expropriation was made by force, with no written papers. Although these changes should simplify the law and make its enforcement easier, the solutions adopted discriminate against the legal owners after 50 years of defiance and abolition of private property. The new regulations are in compliance with a market economy and include buying-selling private lands as a basic element. However, they are not practically discussed by anybody in

Romania. The new rules of the game should have started to work on the basis of an as correct as possible situation, i.e. restoration of land to the legal owners to avoid what had already happened in the buildings sector. The privatization of the State farms (IAS) without a previous judicious restoration is similar to the possibility the tenants have to buy the houses they live in although the legal owners exist.

The forests are mainly owned by the State and with good reasons indeed. The world experience in the field shows that the problem is not property but correct and ecological forestry. This is another drawback of the political approach in Romania. Instead of taking care of a good forestry first by implementing adequate regulations, they adopted privatization rules that stimulated deforestation, both in the sectors owned by State and by private owners or potentially private owners who hurriedly turned their possession to account.

Although the present administration probably considers that the property has been regulated in Romania by passing the buildings law and by changing the law on giving back lands, the result is much below the Euro-Atlantic norms. Some of the provisions in these laws are in total contradiction with the above-mentioned norms. To say nothing of the legislation ambiguity in delimiting the public domain or about the complete confusion in the field of industrial property to be privatized – both major obstacles to reform and to a genuine market economy.

The property issue might remain unsolved. Things can go on in their usual manner. But the expected integration of Romania, supported by almost all the Romanian politicians, should be reconsidered. In the value system of the Euro-Atlantic world property is sacred. We are not sure that this world welcomes Romania, but it is certain that if the latter does not place property in the same value system the former will have the best pretext for making us leave them away.

Likewise, the Romanian politicians could go on in their usual way, but they should hold their tongues and stop making declarations about Romania's Euro-Atlantic integration.

4.2. Role of State: calamitous confusions

The role of State in economy creates a disastrous confusion. Of course, the issue is controversial. Even if the successful market economies accept some main lines in the field, there is a large spectrum of possibilities characterizing the economic-social lives of the respective countries. Practically, the role of State in economy can only be shaped in time.

However, several basic rules of the game should have been established when passing from command economy to market economy and from collective property to private property. Likewise important, a few basic rules should have been established so that the process could not degenerate into dissolution of State and of its institutions. The State, weak and impoverished as it was, failed to fulfill its minimal mission and little by little became the target of systematical devaluing in the name of economic freedoms and stopped guaranteeing the social and political freedoms the population had gained.

Everything started in 1990. While the then opposition seemed more and more enthralled by the vague slogan "Down with the communism!" Iliescu and Roman's NSF found the best way to keep intact the very economic foundations of the past. Pretending to fight against centralization and for reducing red tape they separated the owner-State from the public authority-State. Theoretically, the movement was a correct one. The State should not be the direct manager of economy, as it had proved to be the worst managers of all, mainly in communist Romania. NSF assumed the task of correcting the wrong allocation of resources while the government was to represent the State as a public authority. Economically, the State had a fund-raising role, as it had to collect taxes and to use them for social-cultural and defense expenditures; the economic management of the State organizations should have been the responsibility of their own managing staff. The July 1990 law on the organization of trading companies regulated their very management autonomy. However, the true intention of the post-December power became obvious pretty soon, at the end of the year, when the new public authority-State had to account for the management of the public money. The budget they presented was exclusively one of the public authority-State: the tax incomes and the way that money was spent. The owner-State was simply "forgotten". Not a word about the State property, the most important part in economy that should have been presented in an official report. From then on nothing has ever been said about the owner-State. Nobody ever speaks about it, if anything is sold or how much is spent, if the enterprises are profitable, about the taxes they pay, and how long should the owner-State be supported with public money. Behind this lack of transparency, for which nobody has ever been made responsible, maneuvers of all kind are made: camouflaged subsidization of so many bankrupt industries and lots of thefts.

Maybe the most unfortunate of all the measures initiated by Iliescu-Roman administration was the conception lying at the basis of the privatization process in Romania. Six bureaucratic institutions were in charge of the process: five Private Property Funds (PPF's) and a State Property Fund (SPF). The five PPF's had to manage 30% of the capital of trading companies meant to become the property of the adult Romanians (according to law), a responsibility the PPF's were supposed to hold until the people had got the shares of the respective companies. SPF had to sell the rest of 70% of the trading companies' capital which remained State property until privatization. Even a nonprofessional could realize that such a privatization was neither rapid nor operational, as the above institutions were not interested at all in promoting the process. Privatization meant for SPF its very disappearance and for PPF's, the end of their activities once the people had got their shares. In fact, the post-December privatization institutions were invented in an attempt to centralize and to control the privatization process. Such an attempt – to centralize something naturally meant to be decentralized – could only result in dissatisfaction and restraint and, mainly, in back-stage success.

Even more dramatic, the uncertain statute of SPF, mainly created to represent the owner-State (conceived as a shareholder and not as a responsible owner, as a mere privatization factor of the shares and not as a manager of the State capital to be privatized) initialed a confusion, intentional or not, but detrimental, between the State withdrawal from its position as a manager and that of giving up the owner's authority, a fact having irremediable consequences.

The Vacaroiu government tried a State-based redress of the great mistake made by the Roman government that had granted managerial autonomy to the State enterprises without delegating the management responsibilities, throwing them in a serious authority crisis that dangerously increased corruption, degradation, and embezzlement. By empowering directors without asking anything in exchange (as Roman had done), Vacaroiu was more wrong than right. As they had authority and no obligation, the directors of the State enterprises enthroned a kind of tacit dictatorship of immobility that, under the central approval, almost blocked the impulse of change. More than that, the concern to idle the workers was the government's responsibility while the trade unions were in charge of increasing the directors' own wages. If those directors wanted to set up some parasitic Ltd.'s to sell the products of the State enterprises they managed, they could easily become multi-millionaires or multi-billionaires. Under such circumstances, what was the use of reform or of a fight for reform?

The NPP-NLP-DP coalition struck the final blow. After that, nothing could have been done even if one had tried to.

4.3. Political aggression against business

Another harmful confusion governed the relations between politicians and businesspeople. A serious conflict seemed to exist between private entrepreneurs, more or less as a whole, and politicians, either governing or in opposition, who were blamed for having no interest in stimulating private initiative, in encouraging investments, or in developing economy. It is true that the business milieu in Romania was unfriendly, overburdened with ponderous management and legal procedures, that the legal system proved to be elusive and complicated, taxation high, public administration corrupt and ingratiating, politically dependent and subordinated to the intrusions of the political forces.

Obviously, at the beginning, the businesspeople in Romania chose an indirect approach, supporting the politicians they considered able to promote the business climate and the domestic capital. There is no secret that they directed their support to the politicians governing at a time or another, since they had the power of decision and could be helpful.

As their planes proved often wrong, the entrepreneurs changed their strategy and entered the arena, both because of the serious economic decline and probably because they had no one to rely on. The message was clear: the businesspeople were no longer inclined to credit the politicians who did nothing to change the negative tendencies in economy.

Maybe it was something more. The dependence of economy on politics started to disturb the businesspeople, even those who succeeded in the shadow of the spoils' system or simply used it. The majority of the businesspeople would like something different, although their demands have not been made clear yet, despite the fact that their organizations think they have identified both what they want and what might be done. Some of them, quite a few, are ready to demand no more than the present economy can offer. Some others, quite a lot and quite influential, strive to get facilities that would represent a kind of recapitalization on the State budget account, but impossible to be supported by the State, with rather negative consequences on the economy.

For the time being, all of them agree in blaming politicians both for lack of facilities and for subservience. Obviously, a conflict has appeared and deepened in Romania. Unlike the situation existing in other market economies, the Romanian businesspeople can neither find politicians to take into account their opinions, nor are they politically propelled by the economic circles in order to represent and promote their interests.

The historical experience of capitalism development shows that the change of politicians into business people's spokespersons is an exceptional solution for exceptional circumstances. Otherwise, such a thing is not necessary. A kind of web of relations appears in time among the main groups of economic lobbyists and the main political actors who, within a political and social game generally accepted and respected, ensures the promotion of social and economic interests by their permanent confrontation, by rebalance or lack of balance from one time to another.

There was no time in Romania for such a thing. Just twelve years have elapsed from the events of 1989, when command economy started being replaced by market economy. The present vague relations between businesspeople and politicians should wonder nobody, mainly if we remember the special circumstances in Romania. The political way was the simplest, the most direct, and therefore the one they used.

A lot of politicians are involved in a wide range of economic or connected activities. When the politicians have acceded to political circles, they become interested in economy; the opposite is not very often. Their economic activities – generally started to ensure financial independence as a support for the political act meant to contribute to the nation's welfare – often change the politicians into a kind of prisoners of the cliental network and hinder them in their attempt to identify the real and important problems.

The fluctuating power, following the 1996 elections, has not brought the long expected clarification of the relations between politicians and businesspeople or, more exactly, the relations that could have been beneficial to the economic development. Some aspects are even more complicated and more confused than before whereas some others have been made clear enough, maybe for good, even if they are not to the best advantage of one part or another. Likewise, some other problems still to be solved have emerged and they will probably focus the future web of relations to be settled between businesspeople and politicians.

Mention should be made that the administrations before 1996 saddled the businesspeople with two difficult burdens they had to cope with on a long term, more difficult than anything else they experienced following 1996. The former is the deep hostility of the population, generated by the objective fact that a lot of fortunes had been accumulated in a quasi-illegal manner. The latter is the false impression of the private entrepreneurs themselves that their business could always be conducted under the umbrella of the State, a fact that created a long-term competitive handicap hardly to be removed.

During the first Iliescu administrations, the public authority, irrespective of its segments (police, justice, etc.), let the things develop in their own way. There was no legal system to face the liberty got after giving up command economy and nobody tried to create one. The propensity to breaking laws, few as they were, grew on the one hand when the people realized that nothing could be done without money, and, on the other, when it was crystal clear that those who broke the law were not punished at all. The nation's resources were almost stretched to their limits.

It had long been realized that the only sensible solution for stopping the disaster was privatization. Nevertheless, privatization was either stalled until 1996 or it targeted only populist aspects with no chance of success on a long term. Special facilities were enacted to privatize organizations by offering shares to the staff and to the leadership by the so-called MEBO method. Most of them were unsuccessful because of lack of resources and of the feeble authority of an incorporeal owner. The majority of these organizations did not become more competitive, since they could not be updated, nor could they pay the debts made by the new owners to buy them. The organizations included in the populist program of mass privatization met the same difficulties. Unfortunately, out of varied reasons, the privatization made by selling the organizations did not have a better fate. In many cases, more or less direct facilities were offered (very small prices, preferential credits, etc.). However, following a short effervescence, most of them cracked up. The same lack of the necessary money for privatization was again determining. However, a lack of management ability and the propensity of the new owners to make money very quickly were as many reasons that added to the lack of success.

The suspiciousness of the pork-barrel politics was general. Banks had their own contribution since they granted loans by flouting the basic credit norms. Capitalists thus emerged who could not even say they had started from 100 *lei* and that their entrepreneurial mind did the rest; the generous gifts offered by banks helped them start with billions. Another Romanian originality in the field.

As a matter of fact, during the administrations before 1996, the public money was generously offered to people with more or less entrepreneurial spirit but with a great desire to become rich very quickly through a spoils' system; the nation's resources were simply offered (like in the case of the so-called PPF); credits were given with no guarantee insurance and recuperation prospects; organizations or assets were sold under their value; the nation's resources were stolen; complicity of those responsible for ensuring the observance of laws, etc.

Let us not forget the hostility towards the "privatized", thought to be a kind of highwaymen. Therefore, there is no wonder that the businesspeople or the would-be businesspeople considered that everything was possible and that they deserved everything.

The administration following 1996 contributed a lot to discredit even more the politicians in the eyes of the people. The result of the November 1996 elections clearly showed that the previous governments had been penalized for their passive attitude to the above-mentioned situation. The new administration promised that they would never accept such things and that they would attack, in their words and deeds alike, corruption and lawless.

However, the battle for dividing resources was even fiercer. Owing to the unhappy "algorithm", that represented the key of that administration, the resources and their management were distributed among the allied forces as a function of the number of members they had in the Parliament: the ministries, the jobs in the public administration, in the legal system, in economy, agriculture, and in banks, in the institutions in charge of privatization. The embarrassing show of the hungry newcomers who wanted their share destroyed any hope that "these ones could be different" and stigmatized the whole political class: "they all are equal".

On a short term, the incompetence of the coalition government was disastrous for the Romanian businesspeople. The long-term impact was quite different. The greater the odium against the politicians the lesser the hostility against private entrepreneurs themselves, considered a kind of victims of the former – an important gain for the future. Many of the entrepreneurs did not even realize what had happened. In a short time they were no longer the "bad boys", but the "good ones", a long-term victory worth treasuring. A victory that should be enhanced by strengthening the social function the businesspeople are supposed to confer to their capital.

In the new context, despite the politicians' assault on economy (with less and less success), the businesspeople should avoid any direct involvement in politics for their best interest on a long term. The public image of quite a few successful businesspeople should have no connection with a direct political involvement. However, the deciding influence of the economy on politics might make them follow such a route. A lot of entrepreneurs might not resist temptation and they might consider themselves entitled to govern the country better than the politicians do.

Probably the elections in 2000 were the last ones characterized by a genuine siege of the entrepreneurs to politics. Unless they do not mind their own business there will probably be no professionalism either in politics or in business.

Another long-term positive impact of the 1996–2000 administration was the beneficial natural selection that worked among businesspeople.

The empty bag was an economic reality of the period following 1996. Whoever the winner the situation would have been the same. The cake to be shared was very small and the staggering speed with which it was distributed made it disappear quickly. The unpaid debts along with the domestic and foreign expenditures higher than the incomes did the rest.

An epoch died and it is difficult to think that it would ever come back. The domestic capital has to go on lying on its own forces and on the existing market. The slight balancing of the State accounts accomplished by Ciorbea, then by Radu Vasile, and finally by Isarescu governments (it could have been anybody else's responsibility because the deadline had come) blocked the stipendiary development of the domestic capital. As a matter of fact it was the population who finally paid the money. The consumption decreased and consequently the domestic capital had to face a double difficulty: a more limited access to public money and a shrinking market. A new situation appeared: for the first time, the post-December private capital had to face difficult competitive conditions. The really good ones succeeded. Those used to be offered everything turned to the State and pushed for facilities, mainly in the fields of profit taxation and tariffs which the budget could not support. However, let us suppose that it could. The financing source would be then population, either in a direct way, or in an indirect one. For private entrepreneurs the advantage would be a deceitful one since consumption would decrease even more dramatically. Therefore they could get some financial assistance to produce more but they would not have anybody to buy their products. They have to face reality, difficult as it might be, since their problems have been generated mainly by a lack of market, not of facilities.

The private capital should seriously consider if this kind of facilities represent, under the present conditions, a genuine solution or quite the opposite: the solution could be rather a push for a squeezing budgetary deficit able to eliminate the factor that makes the interests exceed the inflation rate and kills the real economy.

4.4. The private sector should not depend on the State

Should the private sector develop following the market or based on budgetary contributions, as well, a fact that would involve an artificial, but also dangerous dependence on the State?

However, the problem is more general and concerns the relations existing between the private entrepreneurs and the Romanian State, and the rules governing those relations as well. Taking into account the counterproductive experience of Romania, generated by the massive dependence of economy on politics, anything at all that could sanctify or strengthen that dependence should be avoided. The economic framework should move freely and should not be predicated by politics. In a pork-barrel politics like the one existing in Romania this is the only solution. Or, in other words, the Romanian private sector should not rely on the State.

The disastrous tendency of expecting everything from public money – since for a whole decade nobody had to answer for the way it was spent – could be rather... hilarious sometimes. For instance, The National Association of Importers and Exporters in Romania (NAIER) estimated that in 2000 the exporters would have losses higher than one billion dollars caused by the dollar-euro exchange rates. They made the National Bank responsible for their losses since the Bank did not try to protect them by expense accounts of their transactions at *leu* against a basket of currencies including dollar and euro evolutions as well. Their losses were in fact caused by a depreciation of euro versus dollar having no connection at all with the National Bank of Romania. Since their deliveries had mostly western markets and were therefore made in euro, they simply lost.

The introduction of such a basket of currencies is to be considered, but when the euro and the dollar had more or less the same value no Romanian exporter asked for its introduction. Why do not NAIER ask the same thing now, when the euro is much stronger than the dollar? Would they agree to share their benefits with the Bank and with the Romanian taxpayers?

Instead of trying to protect themselves against the currency risks – maybe they do not know how or they are not able to – they preferred to ask the Romanian State to compensate them for their losses. Where form? From the taxpayers, of course! We do not talk here about singular or exceptional situations, like the one mentioned above. The businesspeople push for implementing accounting and tax regulations only in cases of currency fluctuations that interest them. In other words, they claim from the Romanian State to pay for their possible losses by devaluating *leu* against dollar without accepting to give money back when the devaluation is to their advantage.

4.5. A groping dilemma

Another issue concerning the relations between the businesspeople and the Romanian State is the support of the domestic or of the foreign capital. The RDC-DP administration openly preferred the foreign capital, the only one they thought to have the necessary resources and know-how to invest in the Romanian organizations. However, if we want capitalism we should have capitalists as well and we could not rely on the foreign ones only.

A difficult problem since the people can neither be told that they have to close their eyes because we need our capitalists too nor be invited to praise some foreign capitalists who, unlike ours, have had time to make their capital more "moral". A difficult problem, indeed. The problem of supporting the domestic capital is a very controversial one.

May they be taxation and tariffs facilities or others – price- or management-related facilities – the Romanian businesspeople ask for a kind of special treatment, on account of the poor development of the capital and of its feeble competitive force. An equal treatment would lead to a competitive advantage for the foreign capital. It is however obvious that if the Romanian one got a preferential treatment the foreign capital would consider itself discriminated and would choose to stay even farther from Romania than it already does. Strictly economically, Romania is interested to attract the foreign capital that could equip the Romanian organizations and could make them meet the present international standards. Owing to the fierce world competition in the field, special facilities should be provided for the foreign capital so that it might be interested in the Romanian economy.

On the other hand, as long as Romania is bound to observe the programs agreed with IMF and with the World Bank it will not be able to have its own policy in supporting the domestic capital. These programs do not practically include any of the requests of the Romanian businesspeople: taxation facilities, privatization priorities for the domestic capital, and market revival, but a diminution of the internal demand in order to rebalance economy, mainly by reducing the net consumption of external resources. Since there is no solid alternative to the relationships with IMF or with the World Bank, Romania will be forced to apply the programs they imposed. If the businesspeople could find such an alternative it would be salutary. But they ask only ruthless negotiations and even renegotiations of the agreements with IMF and with the World Bank, an unrealistic attitude since these organizations like ruthlessness.

The only request that has a chance at present, as it is not included in the regulations agreed upon with IMF and with the World Bank, is that the domestic capital should be granted certain facilities in privatizing economic organizations and assets. It is this very aspect that the businesspeople should insist on.

The fundamental criterion, at least from the social point of view – and of the public authority if they agree to assume it – in getting these facilities has to become the so-called social function of the capital.

Likewise, the social function of the capital should be the force criterion in selecting those who represent the interests of the businesspeople in their relations with the State, with the political forces, and most of all, when faced with the public opinion.

4.6. Two main issues in Romania: SMO's and football

The statutes of the Small and Medium Organizations (SMO's) are just another problem within the relations between the domestic capital and the Romanian State.

In Romania, there seem to be two issues at the top of the national agenda: football and SMO's. At least in the economic field there is no other issue about which everybody has an opinion. And everybody complains that urgent measures are not taken and that is why nothing can be done in Romania. Because, they say, SMO's are, on the one hand, the very skeleton of economy and, therefore, the key to success, and, on the other hand, the basis of the middle class and, therefore, the guarantee of political and social stability.

Unfortunately, the "football-like" approach is maybe one of the most revealing examples of the way in which the important issues are derided and discredited in Romania. However, such an attitude should wonder nobody since a complex issue is permanently assaulted by interested intercessions, political demagogy, and unaware approaches.

Therefore, such uninspired influences can only lead to confusion when it comes to a necessary policy for promoting the SMO's development *versus* granting them special taxation facilities. This policy should not compulsorily include special facilities for small and medium economic organizations. Since it is absolutely certain that the lending rates granted to those organizations should not be subsidized (because they could confuse the market and involve embezzlement of funds), tax exemption, as a positive discrimination towards the rest of the business milieu, would be the best way for promoting and developing them.

Facilities given to compensate the handicap the SMO's have when compared with the State organizations that are allowed not to pay their taxes and not to repay the credits they have received cannot be an argument. Generalization of such a privilege would solve nothing; quite the opposite, the budget would be even thinner and the State dissolution stronger.

In any case, the solution for the development of SMO's is not the State responsibility and it cannot be waited for from the State. They have to create a competitive sector able to answer the market and its demands, and should not expect the State, i.e. the people to support them.

The tendencies that started in 1997 created a wave of political agitation around SMO's. The then administration was blamed for having bankrupted these organizations, that once used to absorb workforce but turned into a source of unemployment. However, just about 30% of them went out of business each year, a common figure even in countries with a more stable business milieu. As a matter of fact, the closing down of the SMO's in the 1997–2000 interval was not generated by lack of facilities but by a decrease in consumption that severely reduced their market. The greatest majority of the SMO's going out of business were in the trading sector and in services, where they were predominant. The production-related SMO's were mainly closed because the State organizations, their main customers, were in difficulty as well.

Mention should be made that, leaving aside a thin segment working for the population's direct consumption, the SMO's operating in production are, like in many other countries, subcontractors of some greater organizations. As a matter of fact, SMO's are nothing but a legend. The problem is quite different in Romania: because of some economically non-viable units, a solid, efficient, and competitive sector of small and medium organizations has no chance.

The 1996–2000 governments were also blamed for not having supported SMO's with budget money. What would have been the use of those funds is still not clear; there is however no doubt that those organizations would have been unproductively conditioned by public money. The main problem is that SMO's have no money, but it would be absurd to finance them on the account of the taxpayers.

There are mainly four genuine obstacles that block the way of normal bank financing. First, the discouraging interests as a result of the general economic context. Second, at least till now, by their deposits at the National Bank and by investments in government securities the commercial banks could get profits, without being forced to lend. Third, the lack of a proper culture for financing projects (the beneficiaries do not have precise business plans and the banks have not the ability to appreciate chances and to estimate risks). Fourth, the absence of a functional system of collaterals, that is of guarantees (properties or shares) for credits. May the obstacles belong to the economic macro-stabilization or may they be guarantee-related, the solutions must be global and selective facilities should be avoided.

Perhaps the first priority Romania should have in promoting SMO's is to initiate immediately the package of laws regulating the collaterals and to enforce it.

The second priority is to replace the present rigmarole with an adequate legal management framework able to regulate the whole activity of a SMO, since it is set up until it is closed down. To set up an organization in Romania was a very expensive and mainly time-consuming process and to close it down was even more difficult. That is the very reason why there exist more dormant organizations than active ones. A radical change has to take place in accounting, by adopting the British norms that could remove all the indeterminacy in recording incomes, deduction of expenses, tax base, etc.

The third priority is the infrastructure of the business milieu. This objective requires budget funds for financing information and consulting centers, technological parks, where the present or future businesspeople, who have no money for such special activities, could be informed, get assistance in devising a business plan or in asking banks to finance them, or could carry on some activities together, etc.

Therefore, the State should get involved in ensuring a proper business milieu in Romania. It should create the frame and offer the opportunities while permitting the economic organizations to harness the results. The experience has shown that if the State influences the exploitation of the business milieu and mainly if it tries to replace, even positively, the absence of some real opportunities it will be for the worse.

The PSDR administration after 2000 started to improve the SMO's statutes. Unfortunately, the first thing they did was to grant some controversial facilities the positive influence of which was uncertain on a long term. However, short-term political and appropriating considerations had precedence, since the facilities granted to SMO's were just a shield under which certain representatives of the domestic capital could get on the State gravy train. From the propaganda point of view, the emphasis the business people's organizations put on SMO's (as the backbone of a middle class able to stop the non-European polarization in Romania) is quite understandable. Practically, such an action is tricky since the domestic capital is sent to a marginal position in economy. We should not deceit ourselves. Small and medium organizations cannot exist by themselves; they can only survive in relation to great organizations able to ensure markets. SMO's are flexible and more numerous but they cannot carry on research-development programs that should be the key to competition and to success. The Romanian businesspeople should have higher aims and, together with the representatives of the State, they should build up some corporation structures able to face the international competition.

4.7. Trade unions – roots in the past

The trade unions in Romania are far from what they are in the democratic countries with stable market economies, i.e.

indispensable partners in the social contract ensuring a good operation of the economic mechanism and political stability. Of course, the start is difficult, but all kinds of obstacles, mainly political, rise or are raised since for a whole segment of economy the government is both the representative of the employers and the final arbitrator of the social contract. Despite all attempts the government makes to get rid of its former assignment, the trade unions force it to come back, as the only "valid" interlocutor.

The interest of the post-December power to forestall the unity of the trade union movement was quite obvious and had the expected results. Such a policy found fertile ground in the general division of the Romanian society in the first post-December years, but also in the deceitful interests or in the obscure games of some trade union leaders. Quite a lot of trade union leaders stood out then. More often than not the obscure interests of certain political forces and the defense of the people's rights were closely interrelated. The political fluctuations of some trade union leaders, be they conjectural or by somebody's command, created confusion. Some of them got involved in political affairs of the State or even in the public order. The case of Miron Cozma, the leader of the miners' trade unions in Valea Jiului, is already famous: it represented a great shame for the Romanian trade union movement.

It is doubtful that the leaders of some trade union federations or confederations represent solely the interests of the people as they pretend to. In any case, it is certain that they do not stand for so many people and they will never be followed by many hundreds of thousands or even millions at one sign.

The general belief in the trade union leaders and in the politicians as well is badly eroded; they are both very vulnerable.

The politicians are responsible for the difficult situation in Romanian economy: instead of promoting some unpopular measurements (a difficult task indeed) that would have made economy more efficient and more competitive (to stop allocations of resources towards unproductive sectors and to reallocate them towards other activities with better chances) they have thought of their own pockets only and of the easiest way to reach the existing resources, few as they are. Unfortunately, the trade union leaders acted similarly. The position of the trade unions in unproductive sectors living on account of society and of public money is simply embarrassing. The same is valid for the trade unions in the organizations producing poor quality or useless goods. In an open international competition, any failure recorded by such products is a wrench thrown in Romania, the fate of which is demagogically deployed by the above leaders.

The policy of disunity and discouragement of the trade union movement often turned against politicians themselves. The trade union leaders can no longer control numerous spontaneous, illegal strikes and unauthorized street movements, or more serious offences like blocking national roads. Therefore, the government does not have a strong interlocutor able to offer help in finding the best solutions and in enforcing them.

In fact, the most dramatic aspect of all is that the trade unions cannot be the interlocutor the government could rely on when it tries to apply a severe reform program.

Besides the political maneuvers the trade union leaders are involved in, the employees they represent may have different interests depending on the economic sectors they work in. Therefore, their reform-related attitudes may be different.

The trade unions in the trading companies somewhat support the reform since they have to face the pressure of the people pushing to protect their jobs and their incomes against inflation. This protection is the business of the organizations themselves and not of the State budget as it happens in the case of the so-called autonomous (State) companies (a kind of monopolies). It is obvious that the trading companies can do nothing based on the present structures and so they have to accept restructuring and finally privatization.

Those working in autonomous or in national State companies – that own more than half of the capital in industry – have no interest in privatization and restructuring. Quite the opposite, they want to go on like this, under the umbrella of an extremely harmful and badly conceived State protection.

The trade union leaders in these sectors have turned into one of the most retrograde forces in Romania. They took the initiative – sometimes together with certain political forces – of deferring the public utilities privatization for ten years and thus blocked the consensus the European Union requested for the medium-term economic strategy as a condition for starting Romania's integration negotiations. Fortunately, the obstacle could be got through since the European Union did no longer ask for a consensus. However, this attitude cannot be forgotten since the problem is crucial and is not negotiable. At present, public utilities objectively and unavoidably turn from closed sectors into sectors open to competition and privatization is the very way to achieve it. The tendency cannot be stopped, it is present anywhere in the world, and the retrograde forces in Romania will not stop it. As a matter of fact the decision to sell something belongs to the respective owner, in that case to the Romanian State. Therefore, trade unions can only take decisions related to their own assets and public utilities are not theirs.

Of course there existed unsuccessful or fraudulent cases of privatization, but they should not be taken as excuses in the attempt to block the process. If the trade union leaders were really concerned about Romania, then they should ask for the public control of the public utilities privatization, able to ensure transparency, the observance of laws, and benefit so that such unhappy privatization experiences might never happen again.

Unfortunately, these leaders are not concerned about Romania but about themselves. For ten long years they remained the same and they either entered politics or kept their high positions in trade unions.

Trade-unionists should understand that their leaders have not prepared the trade union movement for private property-based economy, a genuine misfortune indeed! For their own survival, the trade union leaders are interested in protecting State property, mainly the monopolies in the field of public utilities, the only place that can perpetuate their survival.

CHAPTER 5

Thefts – the only high figures

The State dissolution, crisis of authority, cupidity of the political class, the complicity of the institutions meant to observe law and to sanction lawlessness, accompanied by the absence of a proper legal framework, ambiguities related to State property and responsibility in State organizations, and also a lax financial-banking surveillance pushed the thefts in Romania to simply abominable pitches – a security risk menacing the survival of Romania as a State and of the Romanians as a nation.

The present paper does not aim at disclosing and punishing the bulk of thefts from the public welfare. The only sensible thing I can do is to itemize the methods and forms of the thefts made by more or less white-collared Romanians.

The thefts of the public money can be classified in two great categories. The former includes the thefts at the margin of the law, either by taking advantage of a legal vacuum or by turning to the best account the ambiguities existing in various regulations. The latter robbed the public money with all the papers in good order.

There exist multiple breaches of the law in force, more often than not politically covered.

It is easy to found out those cases of privatization made by unequivocal breaches of the regulations. However, it is not that easy to find out the starting point when some cliental arrangements are made: undervaluing industrial units or the assets, to the detriment of public welfare. There existed however cases when the undervaluation was so obvious that a bribe suspicion had to be considered. The price itself is rather difficult to be contested, but the undervaluation is hidden behind a multitude of unclear and slippery terms in the privatization contracts. Likewise, a bribe suspicion is irrepressible since these contracts do not include any penalty to be applied if the buyers fail to keep the contract terms. There also exist numerous “indirect” privatizations, when some State assets merge with private assets, with ridiculous undervaluation of the former and fabulous overvaluation of the latter.

The misappropriations of funds are likewise worth mentioning since they can only be made with a political coverage: changes in the destination of budgetary allocations, of some external funds, and last but not least the financing of the political parties could be identified quite easily.

Foundations too make all kind of financial maneuvers on the verge of law. For a while they are tariff- or tax-exempted, so they have become a kind of turntable for embezzlement of funds and fiscal evasion. This is the only explanation why so many foundations exist in a poor country like Romania.

Let us also remind the illegal taking-overs of the buildings in the State ownership, either given on tick or on bribe. The indirect damages caused by selling or conceding land from the State property or assets from the public welfare following sham bids should also be mentioned. The public acquisition law was postponed by Radu Vasile and Isarescu governments, and by Nastase government for a while, although the European Union expressly required it: the law is a stumbling block for the sham bids.

Huge amounts of money, hundreds or even thousands of billions *lei*, were spent on all kinds of certificates for the handicapped or non-handicapped. Because of the tax exemptions the certificates granted, Romania has got more handicapped people than normal ones. The certificates meant to compensate the communist oppressed ones were given to many people who were not even born during those times.

However, customs became the very sanctuary of such thefts, the place where all kind of goods were smuggled, and mainly those having small volumes and a high value: drugs, cigarettes, alcoholic drinks, works of art, etc. Since Brancusi's *Miss Pogany* was smuggled, it is a wonder that they did not smuggle the modules of the Infinity Column yet. The sanctuary offers an in-out access: the cars stolen in the West enter Romania, and other cars, or maybe the same, leave for other places. Who knows? This issue and drug traffic as well is in the hands of the international networks of Mafia. There is a huge tax evasion for imports that nobody seems to notice, and for fictitious exports, when VAT is unjustifiably refunded.

A real disaster is produced by endless financial schemes, some of which have already become notorious. The thefts might seem rather artful for a nonprofessional, but they are in fact very simple and extremely profitable. Let us see some of them. Somebody takes one or more substantial credits, with the agreement of an important and interested official working in the bank, of course; the guarantees are overestimated or fictitious. The debtor refuses to give the money back and the bank proceeds to legal execution but there is nothing left to take. The justice can do nothing since the sums in *lei* become ridiculously small in two or three years because of the inflation in Romania.

Another example: an investment fund, let us say NIF (National Investment Fund), exchanges its investors' money for shares in a good State organization. However, NIF does not do that in a direct way: an intermediary buys the shares at the low market price and the Fund buys from that intermediary at a huge price. Therefore, the books show huge amounts of money paid for that acquisition whereas, in fact, it was rather cheap. The difference, coming from the investors' money, enters the pockets of the Fund's bosses.

And one more example. Several people decide to set up a bank. After that, following some well-directed phone calls, several State organizations move their accounts to the new bank. A shameless publicity, mainly accompanied by promises of higher interests than other banks, attracts some other money from population. The owners take then credits from their bank, directly or through some intermediaries, and gone they are with the money. Alternatively, a new pattern, they arrange the bank failure: the bank depositors – private persons – receive their money from the other banks that cover the guarantee fund while the State organizations receive nothing.

However, the most grotesque case is maybe that of the National Bank, the loser in its relation with the eternally dying but never wound up Dacia Felix Bank. Sever Muresan, the main stockholder in Dacia Felix, placed somewhere abroad the money he had taken from his own bank. That money was mainly investments or the current accounts of some State organizations: CEC, SPF (State Property Fund), and many others. However, the greatest majority of the money came, unfortunately, from the National Bank, under the so-called overdraft, a mechanism used at that time (1995–1995) by the National Bank to automatically cover the differences whenever a commercial bank closed the day with lesser collections than its payments. The cover had a prohibitory interest, of course, but that did not matter since nobody intended to pay it and the goal was to transfer the money abroad. In this way, Dacia Felix sucked in through that overdraft over 1700 billion *lei*, that is at least 10 000 billion *lei* at the exchange rate in the spring of 2001, until the National Bank finally decided to turn off the tap. Obviously, the National Bank never recovered its money back. Out of political and cliental reasons, never disclosed but presumed, the debit of Dacia Felix grew thinner and thinner with inflation, until it almost disappeared, as the court kept postponing to pronounce the bank failure. In the spring of

2001, Dacia Felix owed $60 million to the National Bank from the $400 million when the overdraft stopped. Nastase government interceded, the legal procedure was stopped, and Dacia Felix was taken over by a foreign bank for $22 million. The National Bank had to advise the transaction, i.e. to agree that it had lost about $350 million. It accepted since the money was to be paid by the Romanian people.

Even worse, through procedure artifices and some other actions at the verge of law, all supported by the public authorities in the field, State organizations were sometimes forced to guarantee the collection of funds that were then ransacked. The case of the CEC involvement in the NIF- called theft is the most famous of all. Unfortunately, other cases of indirect guarantees covered huge thefts as well. The absence of a clear intervention of the public authorities that should have warned the population against the risks generated by such dubious affairs unable to offer the gains they had promised, such as Caritas, SAFI, or NIF, could explain why people lost their confidence in the financial system and in the stability of the public finance.

One can easily realize that the so-called material thefts (car stealing, pick pocketing, burglary, breaking into exchange offices or banks, stealing from warehouses and from pipelines, or electricity stealing) focus both on public and private properties. On the other hand, the big felonies aim at public property only. The people protect their own properties, but, alas, those interested in stealing from public property are so many! If in the former category the complicity of some policemen might be suspected, whereas the latter must involve corruption at higher levels: those trying, hearing, and determining the cases, officials, and high officials.

The stealing from public funds with documents in apparently good order are by far the most insidious and misleading.

The archives of the big organizations must have lists of the State guarantees offered for financing some commercial contracts: should the beneficiary of the credit fail to give the money back, the debt would be paid from public funds. Since such lists refer to public funds, they should be made public! People might see that, besides some justified guarantees such as those for credits of the electricity company (meant to finance some power imports) there are lots of other guarantees nobody knows why for. Why should public funds be spent for the private Sofitel Hotel or for the World Trade Center Complex? Why should the commercial contract for financing the five-star Marriott Hotel have guarantees from the State? Do those hotels have any social or strategic significance?

A complete list of the credits for bankrupt organizations and affairs might reveal situations in which not only political criteria, but also appropriating ones are involved. In fact, Bancorex and Agricola Bank failed because of the money spent with such credits. More than that, the Romanian taxpayer had to pay these so-called non-performing credits (credit losses) of about $3 billion since they became part of the public debts.

Finally, yet importantly, there is another “fascinating” affair: AVBA (the Agency for Valuing the Bank Assets). When the public debts took over the non-performing credits from Bancorex and Agricola Bank, the debts were transferred to AVBA that was supposed to make them profitable, meaning to sell them with a price reduction, so that the State may recover at least a part of its expenses. The affair is fascinating because if the debtors make their best arrangements they can buy their own debts for just some percent and remain then crystal clear, with good money in their pockets. Therefore, they become respectable businesspeople at the expense of the stupid taxpayers who have to pay for their schemes.

Two cases have already become famous. The former: the financial schemes of Mr. Paunescu. More than $180 million were credited from Bancorex for various projects that endorsed the loans among them to the paroxysmal situation when credits where guaranteed with shares of hotels that had not been bought yet. The affair was extinguished through AVBA for just $20 million, when a company from Luxembourg bought it. The same stupid Romanian taxpayer paid the $160 million difference. The latter case is Mr. Catarama's financial arrangement: credits of about $17 million were guaranteed for a building that cost $4–5 million, but was appraised, with the creditor's agreement (!), for $24 million. Finally, AVBA took over the building and Mr. Catarama was absolved from $17 million. It was very ingenious, was it not? On a whole, AVBA recovered about 15% of the value of the debits it had to administer and the same poor Romanian taxpayer paid the rest of 85%.

Such cases demonstrate neither Paunescu's and Catarama's special ingenuities nor even their guilts, but the complicity of some officials in the respective State structures. Obviously, such fraudulent schemes could not have been possible if the managers and other officials in Bancorex had not accepted credits of hundreds of millions dollars to be guaranteed for shares already bought by the debtor or a $4-million building be appraised for $24 million! Likewise, the fraud called NIF could not have been possible if the irresponsible Camenco Petrovici had not involved CEC in a guarantee contract and if officials in the Ministry of Finance, members of the CEC Management Council, had not advised investments of the organization as an NIF investor and as a

SOVINVEST (the organization administering NFI) stockholder.

The people should also be shown the list containing the rescheduling and remissions of the debts, mainly of those made by the State, but not only. However, such a list will never be made public and the honest taxpayers are practically turned into imbeciles.

Each condition under which export premiums were offered should also be analyzed: who was entitled to receive them and why; likewise, the import credits in exchange for fees that filled a lot of pockets.

Let us not forget the politically tolerated parasitic companies. The most grotesque situation exists in the State metallurgical aggregate works, all bankrupt, but all supporting private parasites. In 2000, because of such anomalies, 70% of the steel and cast iron exports were private, although the iron and steel metallurgy in Romania is 100% State-owned. In other words, some work and pay, whereas some others export and take the currency. If this is privatization, then we do better without it!

It is useless to say that all these ways of ransacking public funds with documents in apparently good order cannot be possible without the involvement of the high officials, of the political class itself. As long as the government officials, be they left or right, do nothing against the thefts from public funds the people will refuse to believe that poverty is only caused by an inefficient economy. Although this is the main explanation, the people will know that they are poor because of the thefts.

Rapid and efficient privatization seems the only possible solution for saving what has remained of the public welfare.

If the government, irrespective of its color, were genuinely interested in facing these thefts it should start by assessing the losses from the public funds for 11 years. However, we think that the loss is so huge that the government will either give up or take a gun.

CHAPTER 6

Fewer people, higher poverty

The thefts from public funds have led to unprecedented polarization in the Romanian society: a few people have become very rich and others, more and more numerous, very poor.

During the Romanian transition, the saddest and maybe the most compromising post-December phenomenon took place, since it was associated with the market economy itself: following the pork-barrel politics, a few people became rich in a short time, by breaking the law and defying the largest part of the population.

Beyond the objective absence of some laws that should protect the population against such a phenomenon involving massive rummage of public funds and beyond the complicity of the representatives of the control and legal bodies, the objective basis of the phenomenon was the huge difference between market demand and offer. Alternatively, in simpler words: an excess liquidity, in *lei* of course, beyond any imagination in a normal economy.

The situation was inherited from Ceausescu when both the unemployment and the price safety valves were blocked. Under those conditions, the inefficient economy explosively accumulated inside the closed system, its main manifestation being lack of products in the market and a flagrant lack of cover in products and services of the monetary demand.

When the Iliescu–Roman team took over the power, goods and services covered only 14 *bani* in one *leu* in the market. Even a nonprofessional can realize that an explosion could have been avoided only by opening the safety valves. Taking into account the non-uniform distribution of the excess money, the balance could have been reached by a four- or fivefold rise in prices with no raise in wages. Iliescu-Roman did nothing of the kind. Quite the opposite, out of political and electoral reasons they acted uneconomically and converted Ceausescu's ex investment allowances into wage raises. In this way, the already existing lack of balance in the market was aberrantly amplified and the premises for starting the reform were compromised.

In the fall of 1990, when Roman government finally decided to start the reform, goods covered only 9 *bani* in 1*leu*! How did Iliescu-Roman team try to face the fantastic lack of balance? Was it by correcting it? No way! They tried to solve it by the so-called partial liberalization of prices. It was a price liberalization of goods only, without including interests and exchange rates.

Was it by mistake or, as they claimed, to ensure social security? Was it just to ensure a rapid enrichment or their political clientele? Let us say it was a mistake. It is certain that it was not social security.

The artificially created market by maintaining a higher demand than the domestic offer was, in fact, the very source of the post-December nouveaux riches' prosperity. That was the cow they kept milking systematically, with nothing to worry about. They could sell the few existing goods increasingly expensive because of the demand, artificial as it was.

If the artificially maintained excess had not existed, the Romanian society would have been now more equitable: the State welfare would not have been ransacked, the population would not have been impoverished and, mainly, the Romanian economy would have been healthier since the businesspeople would have been directed to production, without having to restrict to commerce only.

However, the main link between the money excess in the market and the nouveaux riches' prosperity was the import. Because of the poor domestic production in almost all branches, mainly of consumer goods, and of the excess monetary demand, artificially maintained, almost all post-December rich people were importers.

Economically, it is simply inconceivable that in a country with small incomes all the rich people be importers! That emphasizes the artificial character of the domestic demand that permitted the sale of all the imported goods. Had the money excess not existed the imports – more expensive – could have not been sold and thus the present disaster would not have been so huge because the difference between exports and imports would have been lower.

The phenomenon might have not been quite "natural" altogether: the first negative signal of the partial price liberalization that came in 1991–1992 was totally ignored. The gradual price liberalization triggered an inverse and extremely expensive subsidy: of the products already liberalized at the expense of those liberalized later. The socially uninteresting products, the imported ones included, were allowed to absorb a part of the economy and of the population incomes, whereas the production basis of the socially interesting goods themselves was severely affected.

The people had to bear the consequences whereas they thought they were protected by government subsidies. In reality, the devastation of the State budget rapidly suffocated social expenses and finally stopped the subsidies for the main consumer goods and services.

Despite the obviously negative consequences, the policy of the excess monetary demand continued for several years, mainly by pegging the *leu* rate: since the prices of some imports were extremely diminished the importers were granted huge advantages at the expense of the official economy.

The permanent economic reduction, money and budget decreases, the high burden of the non-functional sector, along with shameless thefts from public funds led to a dramatic increase in poverty, much below the European standards.

In a public report of 2001, the World Bank, using the same criteria for the whole ex-communist area, appreciated the poverty increase rate in Romania to be one of the highest and most concerning of all. The number of the poor Romanians was estimated to be of about 9.3 million at the end of the 1990s: 41% of the population. The percent systematically increased and it almost doubled: in 1996, the poor people had represented 19.8%.

Such figures are never met in Europe. More dramatically, the number of the population decreased with increase of poverty. Generally, population increases with poverty in other continents. Romania's case is strange and maybe unique: poverty increased dramatically despite the huge emigration rate and decrease in birth rate.

Since, out of political reasons, no pertinent analyses were made before 1990, Romania seemed to have not been faced with poverty. Nevertheless, poverty existed but it certainly had not reached the present absolute values. The Gross Domestic Product was higher then and much more equitably distributed than nowadays when very few get very much whereas very little is allotted to the greatest majority.

The result is the failure of the Romanian transition: if economic increase had existed, the piece of cake to be distributed would have been larger. The economic failure is mainly visible in the very fact that giving up the egalitarian, communist repartition, Romania estranges from a European model of capitalist society and seems to follow a South American one, with no middle class; just poor and rich people.

The poverty has affected the biological rate of reproduction. In1995–2000, the birth rate reached the lowest level in the 20th century. The same poverty lies at the basis of the massive emigration as well. In ten years, Romania's population decreased with 800,000, following legal and illegal emigration and low birth rate too.

Return to the village in an attempt to live a better life, far from the outskirts of the dying cities and towns, is another phenomenon caused by the deepening poverty. The black labor solution should wonder none; black economy ensures the very survival of the Romanians and without it very serious social instabilities could appear.

More than half of the poor in Romania are working people and that is one of the most concerning and horrible aspects of poverty in this country. This very fact emphasizes the failure of the Romanian economy and the lack of economic performance. The only solution left would be a substantial and long-lasting economic recovery.

CHAPTER 7

Tragic comedy of the "social component"

The funny thing in the post-December Romania is that while the officials pretend to govern following a "social component" of economy and society, that "social component" has become increasingly insubstantial, as proved by the very reality facing us.

A retrospective analysis shows that since the "social component" has turned from an aim into a mean and very often into a political slogan, it might have been at least one of the main explanations of economic stiffness.

Immediately following 1989, Mr. Iliescu and his administration played a populist card just to leave the impression of their dedication to the general cause and resorted to all kind of measurements, economically unsustainable, meant to gain people's goodwill. Thus, he artfully speculated the communist hatred against the "ex's": great owners of land and of factories. Therefore, he called the miners in Bucharest and used them against the "ex's" and against the opposition – against all those who were against him. He promised the people that he would take care of them like nobody else before and he won the elections. He left the impression that he was one of them and he succeeded in having no counter candidate for several years. Finally, he deliberately left aside the target-goal that was supposed to be Romania's destination: he did not want to be the leader who, after a 50-year-communist dictatorship, would direct Romania to capitalism.

When, after years of deliberate silence, Mr. Iliescu and his people realized that they had to say something, they invented the objective of the "social market economy", a term found in the battery of the western social-democracies, with no relevance for the Romanian realities whatsoever. Using this concept, they tried to soften, out of social reasons, the inequality effects generated by an economy working in the conditions of market mechanisms. However, as Romania had not an economic basis for social democracy the officials kept becoming richer and richer while the people were poorer and poorer. Market economy cannot exist in Romania as long as private property does not prevail. Only when the private sector is predominant in Romania a certain market economy model could be chosen. It might be a "social" one as well! However, a "social market economy" coming from communism and not from capitalism risks to fail in ensuring the long referred to "social component": an efficient economy based on private property, able to create something that could be then equitably distributed following social criteria. This risk has already appeared in Romania. Actually, the blocking off of the reforms toward a market economy closes the way to better performances and therefore nobody can expect higher resources for financing the long-sounded "social component."

Therefore, while Mr. Iliescu and his acolytes won the elections and strengthened their positions, deceitfully claiming to have followed the Scandinavian social-democratic pattern, the Romanian society followed an opposite direction, to the South American pattern, characterized by a most dramatic social discrepancy.

The so-called right governments that interrupted for a while the management of the "social component" preachers recorded a serious economic failure that permitted the latter to easily regain power and direct Romania to a non-European capitalism.. Ironically and tragically, Romania at the turn of the millennium repeats its own inter-war experience: the same 70–80% people living in poverty are this time faced to a purely Romanian "bourgeois-landlord" stratum, despite the hard attempts of the left to defy the old NPP representatives' references to those years.

This time, the new dynasties are the descendants of the ex-communist nomenclature and of the late secret services. Business can only be made with money, acquaintances, and information and very few except those already mentioned are able to get them. Although having a different origin and pretending to have left- or social-democratic orientation, the new "bourgeois-landlord" class has the same proclivity towards luxury, expensive cars, and vacations in Paris or on the French Riviera.

That is the reason why in a poor country with underdeveloped economy there is such a flourishing market for costly products, huge mansions, casinos, etc. In these conditions, one of the consequences affecting the chance of development is the loss of the capital social function: it is used for gaining rapid profit – more often than not speculatively – instead of financing productive activities with long-term gains and with important social impact.

There is no wonder then that nobody in Romania promotes products, houses, or restaurants for people with average incomes, although those proved to be the key to success in all the other countries. Such a concern cannot exist since there are not such people.

The absence of the middle class means a small domestic market and hence poor prospects, since economy lacks a real development foundation.

CHAPTER 8

The controversial role of the international financial organizations

Romania is therefore an economic and social failure: in 12 years it has not even been able to reach the GDP it had during communism and social polarization has reached dangerous and embarrassing dimensions. In these conditions, how could be appreciated the role of the international financial organizations involved in programs having the above-mentioned results?

There are voices claiming that all the troubles of the post-December period are, in a way or another, caused by the international financial organizations, at least indirectly through the conditions they imposed on Romania. On the other hand, there are other voices appreciating that the few steps made are the exclusive contribution of those institutions both by the programs they recommended and mainly by pushing the Romanian officials who act solely under a foreign spur.

The reality is rather complex. There is only one certain thing. The receipts IMF and World Bank prescribed for Romania cannot be separated from the economic and social results Romania got on its way to transition. One cannot say that everything they recommended was perfect and the only ones responsible for the economic and social failure in Romania were its uninspired administrations or, according to some cynical opinions, the psycho-social or psycho-cultural data of the Romanian people.

The programs IMF and the World Bank recommended for Romania had both necessary and correct targets. However, the indications for reaching them were not the ideal ones for the existing conditions in the Romanian economy. (They might have been good in other countries, although no important success has been known up to now).

Taking into account Romania's specific situation, they should have insisted on the gradual reduction and elimination of the non-functional sector and on conditioning the acceptance of each external financing on direct and indirect measurements taken in that direction. Instead, IMF chose to impose programs of budgetary and financial restrictions that failed to reach their targets and affected the rest of economy while the non-functional sector survived under a political umbrella. In this way, the "neuter" policies the international financial organizations recommended for Romania damaged mainly the healthy economic sector.

Trying to impose some programs of macroeconomic stabilization in a non-market economy, through market instruments, IMF did not probably realize that the non-functional sector inherited from command economy could only be liquidated through market instruments, during a generation, and that no rush could avoid the administrative means. Therefore, the non-functional sector is in its place and economy has been left fewer and fewer instruments to eliminate the non-functional sector.

Essentially, the main dysfunction of the IMF–World Bank programs has grown deeper with each passing year. IMF keeps insisting on the so-called macro-stabilization, i.e., on low inflation and relative stability of the national currency. However, without restructuring the real sector of economy these goals cannot be reached, correct and necessary as they might be. Restructuring means demolition and building alike. The loss-generating companies can only be shut down when economic-social alternatives have been created. Investments of about 17–18% of GDP might ensure survival, but no building up or development.

That is why the IMF and World Bank programs cannot ensure economic success. IMF insists on macro-stabilization but it cannot be achieved without restructuring that, in its turn, cannot be achieved without money. Neither IMF nor Wide Bank gives the money and they hypothetically bank on private money that would come following their guarantees. However, since it is certain that private investors will do nothing without guarantees from the mentioned organizations it is less certain that they will do anything if those organizations accept to guarantee. Other countries in transitions experienced the same situation: they succeeded only following a serious involvement of the western capital. Unfortunately, Romania is not among them.

Meanwhile a vicious circle has been created: on the one hand, with no domestic resources, the government in Bucharest badly needs IMF's accept to get some external financing; on the other hand, IMF and World Bank's programs have not been economically successful and they are not a guarantee for attracting the long-expected private financing from abroad.

The two foreign organizations keep insisting on economic sanitation – that is no doubt necessary – and completely skip the construction side that they leave at the discretion of some hypothetical foreign private investments. Since domestic resources for reconstruction are completely absent and foreign investments are simply hypothetical, social and political availability along with the economic resources for the necessary sanitation in economy will soon cease to exist.

CHAPTER 9

A simple explanation: too much stealing, too much poverty!

"Too much stealing, too much poverty" is the simple explanation of the vote of November 26, 2000. Both the vote in 1996 and in 2000 was negative. In 1996, the people had voted against PSDR for almost the same reasons; in 2000, they voted against the Democratic Convention and mainly against its symbol, the representatives of the NPP. However, it was not their incompetence that the population sanctioned them for, but their greed that was not a bit less than that of their predecessors. In fact, the economic failure was so huge and the price the population had to pay for that failure so big that the majority of voters simply forgot the past and turned into saviors those responsible for the economic failure of the previous six years. More than that, quite a lot preferred GRP (Great Romania Party) and Vadim Tudor who offered no solution for the present state of things but were the only ones who promised to stop thefts. The votes for GRP expressed the revolt against *the authority*'s helplessness, indifference, or even complicity related to the thefts and illegalities never punished. Likewise, the vote of 2000 penalized the South American type polarization in Romania that, besides the delay in starting the necessary reforms, kept Romania away from Europe and from its economic and social models. Finally, the vote of 2000 revealed the disastrous political, social, and economic situation existing in Romania at the beginning of the new millennium.

CHAPTER 10

Demonizing reform

The long-delayed reform is completely demonized: it is not even considered a "necessary evil" but "the evil." It has been expected for too many years and finally people have turned completely against it. Now, even if one absurdly admitted that the politicians thought about it, they would have to face against the population's will. Unfortunately, neither politicians nor people think of reform and there are serious doubts that it would ever be applied in Romania despite the fact that it is badly needed. Reform is assimilated here with pains only and, taking into account the results, with useless pains. Now it is difficult to tell the people that the pains were useless for the very fact that reform was not made, since the politicians already told them that they had to experience pains in the name of the reform itself.

The situation is tragic and Romania is doomed to remain in its present state, with no hope to ever get out of it. PSDR has been governing since 2001 and they have not started reform. In fact, that is the reason why their credibility has increased. Unfortunately, if PSDR does not start to do something there is no other hope. Added to its multiple misfortunes, Romania has remained without opposition as well. The existing one is totally divided in a practically irreconcilable cleft, a situation speculated by the PSDR administration. In fact, GRP agrees with PSDR approach, although it is doubtful that they will ever be able to ensure a decent living standard in Romania, to say nothing about the European integration. The so-called democratic opposition can only keep silence or PSDR would remind them of their disastrous administration when they did nothing of the kind. NLP pretends to be a reformist but, when they governed, they preferred to let reform wait and followed their cliental interests. On the other hand, DP boasted about reform just to get some economic ministries – a diversion the voters penalized rather quickly. For DUMR, reform means nothing else but plates, legal proceedings and education in Magyar; as PSDR knows it too well, they grant DUMR everything and get their support in everything, the reform skipping included.

CHAPTER 11

Economy – an unsuccessful hybrid

The unhappiest product of the so-called transition in Romania is the unsuccessful hybrid between the official economy and the market one that appeared in 12-year time and is ready to take over the drawbacks from both of them.

Market economy can be nothing but a failure when some or just one of its main component parts is missing. They are missing all right in Romania: inflation explodes if the unemployment safety valve is closed and the price safety valve is the only one open. Without a capital market, the investment funds have overturned. With no competition, it is not demand and offer that regulates prices and allocation of resources but the blackmail of the market monopolist positions, while credit alters its function. However, the risk of compromising the private sector is the most serious of all. It is not the fact that some get rich while some others get poor that compromises the private sector, but the fact that so many get rich by theft and corruption. In the meantime, the capital they have accumulated is not used for investments and thus it loses its social function: it is spent for expensive cars and luxurious mansions, for provoking eccentricities, for some other useless activities, and even for illegal capital exports.

As some of the market economy main components are missing, it cannot function properly and can only lead to social polarization.

Romania at the beginning of the 21st century has kept the same old economic structures but has experienced a dramatic alteration of the new market mechanisms and institutions; practically its economy is not better than that before 1989. As the production structures have remained unchanged, they can only allow the same old performances and therefore the same standard of living. The difference from the western countries is even greater and so is the one from the Central-European countries.

Romania is again Europe's laggard. The discussion about Romanian industry being or not scrap iron has proved useless since 12 years have already elapsed and everything has become old fashioned in the meantime. The fact is that the Romanian industry has not been updated for more than 20 years: at the beginning of the 1980s, when the external debt started being paid in advance, all the imports of modern equipment and technologies were stopped.

Since the few existing resources are wasted to maintain the non-functional industries and the rest is sucked dry by the transition "parasites," there is no chance of development. Romania, having the same old industry and the same old export offer, is not at all prepared to face the international competition and will remain even farther behind.

The Brussels Commission of the European Union practically dots the i's when appreciates that Romania is not "a functional market economy" yet.

What else might be added besides some more explanations and appreciations? Perhaps the exact picture of the Brussels Commission Report on the Romanian economy and on the other related sectors: macroeconomic frailness; weak progress of the structure reforms; instability of public finance; low level of foreign investments; institutional disaster; corruption that undermines the legal system and affects both economy and the confidence in public authorities; inability to administer the irredeemable funds from the European Union, etc.

The hybrid born out of a frail market economy and a dying official economy cannot be a functional market economy. In Romania the increase in prices goes hand in hand with diminishing demand; the highest wages are those in the loss-generating organizations; the electricity bills exceed the average monthly wages; the State budget has to support all kind of unusual expenses (bankrupt companies or thefts in the banks) and can no longer assign funds for financing education, national defense, health, or public order. Romania is also the country where those who do not pay their taxes are the smart ones since the State reschedules their debts or even forgives them altogether, whereas the suckers who pay their taxes are ridiculed. The banking system in Romania has too much money whereas real economy misses them. It is also in Romania that the pension budget is supported both by the State budget and by the unemployment aid fund although it has nothing to do with any of them. Why? Because the people have to retire in advance to avoid thus unemployment.

Here you are just some of the anomalies in Romanian economy. Because of them, it cannot have "a functional market economy" yet.

CHAPTER 12

Facing atypical problems

Hybrid economy, half measures applied in reform, along with the very hard to change inertial economic structures inherited from communism have forced Romania to face some atypical problems in its way to development.

The first of them, and maybe the most serious of all, is generated by the fact that massive demolition has to precede a new construction. For development in general, the problem is atypical although it is typical for the whole ex-communist space. Unfortunately, it has a higher degree in Romania than in the other countries in the South and Central Europe both because Romania inherited from communism the most orthodox command economy and because the reforms were delayed so much. Nowadays the part to be demolished and normalized represents a higher percent than in any other ex-communist country in the area.

Romanian economy has to get rid mainly of the State industrial organizations, non-functional and with no markets. Unfortunately, it has no longer the money it needs. It is only a massive and direct foreign investment that could relax constraints through a change in sequentialities, i.e. by creating first the economic and social alternative that could become a basis for the necessary demolition in the future.

Economically, Romania has to face the typical problems of the underdeveloped countries whereas demographically, it has to face the characteristic problems of the industrially developed countries. The rather irreconcilable problems and the opposed character of the measures to be taken can create major economic or social breaches almost impossible to avoid.

Objectively, on account of its economic underdevelopment, Romania cannot have the financial resources to ensure concomitantly birth stimulation, economic protection of mothers and children, and protection of the more and more numerous old people. The phenomenon of the "ageing" population has not created dramatic problems up to now: it only existed in the developed countries that were able to solve it.

Because of its economic incapacity Romania could become – in a few years – the first example of capitulation in front of the "ageing" population phenomenon. Since the retired people are 17% more numerous than the average in the developing countries, the pension scheme in Romania will be under the permanent pressure of the relative decrease of the pensions as related to wages.

For many decades from now on Romania will have to face another atypical problem. From the viewpoint of the dimension and structure of its land property, Romania has returned to the 1950s period in the history of European economy. Therefore, it will have to resume the unavoidable historical process of concentrating and centralizing land and capital in agriculture while providing workforce from that sector in a period of industrial restructuring. That involves redundancy rather than workforce absorption. Objectively, social tensions will appear but they cannot be responded economically. For the time being the process is blocked but the longer the blockage, the more dramatic the consequences will be. For at least a decade from now on, industry will not be able to absorb the workforce in excess. Consequently, besides agriculture, industry will furnish workforce as well, an atypical situation that will raise major social problems. On the other hand, services cannot develop without a solid industrial infrastructure able to offer a market for them.

Some budgetary constraints acting in a kind of vicious circle generate another atypical problem: the political forces in Romania want to ensure the kind of social security typical of the developed countries with the Gross Domestic Product of an underdeveloped country.

History of economy shows that the countries that chose development did not pay much attention to social security. The United States themselves do not bother much about social security. When the Western European countries started their development several decades ago, they did not sacrifice the prospect of development in favor of social security. The latter was but the natural consequence of the economic development. The Asian countries had neither the social security problem nor the trade unions one. Therefore, the resources could be directed with no constraint towards investments; the results appeared after 15–20 years when social security meant new jobs and decent incomes.

Following 1989, Romania has always chosen social security to the prejudice of the investments, leading to the relative decrease of the budget that can hardly offer the development resources and will finally fail to ensure the type of social security it wants to promote. Irrespective of the political desires, the social security in Romania must be different from that in the developed countries and it should focus mainly on protecting the poorest members of society.

CHAPTER 13

Survival through black economy

The hybrid Romanian economy can only survive due to its black component.

A study of the Romanian black economy ordered by the US Treasury at the end of the 1990s showed that Romania got an economy parallel to the official one representing about half of the latter, valued as such by GDP and official statistics. Although the study disclosed an open secret, the Romanian analysts and even politicians paid due attention to it.

In fact, an official RSI (Romanian Intelligence Service) report had shown, several years before, that black economy represented in Romania 40–45% of GDP.

However, the American study is more credible since it shows both the phenomenon evolution and comparisons with significant international situations.

The study starts from the premise that if the cash in circulation and bank deposits have divergent evolutions – more exactly if cash increases and deposits decrease – black economy widens, since its vehicle is cash only.

The importance of the American study and the attention paid to it justifies an analysis of its estimations and conclusions.

For the sake of reality, the term "parallel economy" should be used. A large part of the economic activities – maybe half – taking place outside official economy are not "black" meaning "secret" or illegal; they are simply unaudited. Activities in the agriculture, buildings in villages, sales in the village markets, or various services in towns are somewhat included in GDP, but not at their real dimensions, difficult to be estimated. The rest are illegal activities (contraband, money laundering, black labor, blackmails, etc.). The American study evidences an increase of this unauditedeconomy in Romania, but it does not show if the increase is due to the illegal segment or to the legal but unaudited one.

However, their methodology offers solid ground for some conclusions. For instance, the cash-bank accounts ratio is not useful in appraising the unaudited movements in villages, inhabited by about half of the Romanians. Lately, the economic ratios there have significantly moved towards a kind of natural economy, governed by barter relations having no connection with either market or money.

On the other hand, the American study emphasizes that the parallel Romanian economy is largely import-based because of the decrepit productive system in the official economy. Let us make a comparison with the parallel export-based economy in Turkey that succeeded in the 1990s to absorb huge, unofficial resources from the ex-communist countries, mainly from Romania, through tourism-covered flows.

However, the system of parallel economy has in Romania a relatively stable local basis ensured by selling imported goods. The money got is used for new imports and it is not necessarily placed abroad. The American study does not mention this aspect, but estimates the import-based component to represent two thirds. That means that the domestic component of the parallel economy in Romania would represent just one third – an entirely nonrealistic appraisal.

If that internal component had been so small the parallel economy would not have known such an extension: when the consumption decreased so drastically at the end of the 1990s, the imports would not have been so huge and the very factors of the black economy would have left Romania for other evasion havens.

The American study signaled that the Romanian black economy reached the margin of the civilized economic system and therefore it cannot be eligible for that system. However, the study says nothing about the phenomenon through which the Romanian balance of payments succeeds to finance its deficit with official credit inflows and lesser investments than the deficit. That is how parallel economy, included in *Errors and Omission,* contributed to finance the deficit of the external current account in the 1990s. Anyhow, parallel economy, representing at least one quarter of the total, comprises: collections from unaudited exports, taxes for undervalued or illegal goods transiting Romania, commissions for money laundering, etc. Real money is involved here since they generate real imports.

We like it or not, parallel economy plays a major role in Romania. It is however difficult to say if the official economy was crushed by the parallel one or, quite the opposite, weaker and weaker as the former became, it made place for a flourishing parallel one that took over a part of its functions as well.

One should wonder however about the lack of destabilizing social movements. The explanation is simple: parallel economy ensures survival of more than two million people. The way in which parallel economy finances part of the foreign deficit is another example of the way it succeeds in helping Romania not to blow up.

Of course, parallel economy cannot be praised but one should be aware that the absorption of its activities by the official one is only possible when the latter is strong enough to do it. Unfortunately, we are far from that.

CHAPTER 14

If only Romania were a "market place"!

Economically and socially, the failure of the Romanian transition resulted in the country's marginalization abroad. Maybe the most characteristic aspect of the Romanian transition was that its economy – created and developed within an almost total isolationism – was not at all adapted to the domestic and foreign liberalizations made: monetary, commercial, or currency-related. Therefore, it was not able to face the direct competition entailed by such liberalizations.

In 11 years, the Romanian GDP decreased by one fourth meaning that although the country have external debts of $11 billion, the money was used, directly or not, to finance a higher people's consumption than allowed by its economic performances.

Eleven billion dollars in eleven years or, in other words, one billion each year. Although at present one billion dollars is not such a big amount of money, it is for Romania taking into account the poor state of its economy. The workforce in Romania is very cheap, so that social peace can be cheaply bought. However, this situation cannot last endlessly. If economy does not change, some "external sponsors", willing to finance a purchase of the social peace, have to be found each time. If, out of political and election reasons, the wage raises are not reined back, then Romania will need even greater external resources for the people's wages. The currency paid for the social peace will be higher and higher.

During 1992–2000 the wage increase was substantially higher than the *leu* devaluation meaning that the external resources used had to be higher. Therefore, an equal living

standard could be maintained only by increasing the dependence on net currency inflows from abroad each year.
Taking into account the present situation of the Romanian economy and its position within the world economy, Romania is far from a genuine "market place", a collocation totally unfit for such a decrepit economy at the margin of the international competition.

The thesis was backed by PSDR itself when it was in opposition between 1996 and 2000. Then it used to accuse the governing parties for having readily accepted the recipes of the international financial bodies that simply turned Romania into a market place for the western economies.
However, the supporters of such a thesis hardly take into account the realities of the contemporary world economy.

The world division into "bases of production" and "market places" is already history. Economically and politically, it belonged to colonialism; technically, it was a reality of the classical industrialism. The countries in the centre of the system largely developed on the basis of the raw materials exploited in the countries at the system margins. Therefore, the latter were simply sources of raw materials and markets. The mechanism of the colonial exploitation itself consisted in forcing the countries at the margin of the system to export their raw materials to the countries in the center of the system where they were processed and partly sold in the latter. That was the main reason why the liberation of the colonies focused on regaining national control of the raw material resources and on the attempt to create their own processing bases.

Between the two world wars, the countries in the centre sang after another fashion and they are as strong and influential as ever. Nowadays, the marginal countries are, economically, even farther from the center and the distance is almost impossible to be reduced. The transfers of resources among countries have got huge dimensions whereas the transfer schemes are different. Technology has changed everything. The center has the technological initiative and has adapted the world economic structures and relations to the new demands. As a controller of the modern technologies it has strengthened its leading role within the world economy. Now, it is the marginal countries that invite the center to exploit their resources. They simply do their best to attract investments from the central countries. Each country can develop its production base as it likes provided it has got the adequate technology and finds a market for its products. However, the countries in the center control both technology and markets. The center keeps research-development, technologies, financial services, etc. for it while production, mainly the energy-consuming industries, or the polluting ones, are the responsibility of the marginal countries. Nowadays, "market place" means purchase power and a country having a low purchase power cannot be a "market place"!

With almost no mineral resources left, with its oil and gas resources almost drained, Romania could not be a "market place" even if the old days of classical industrialism and colonialism came again. Nothing is left, therefore nothing can be taken and it cannot be a market place for the end products from abroad.

Romania does not lack the productive capacity for turning to account its resources. Quite the opposite: it has too much productive capacity for its domestic resources. Romania is an importer and not an exporter of raw materials. The main problem facing Romania is that the excess of its productive capacity characterizes sectors and activities that were truly representative of the classical industrialism. Objectively, they are in decline at present. The Romanian products are either uninteresting, or qualitatively poor, or not competitive, or all of these drawbacks together. This means that both its domestic resources and those bought from abroad with so much difficulty are poorly used and they cannot enter foreign markets. Romania hardly exports about $10–11 billion each year.

Therefore, the payment capacity is very low as compared with the present international standards and Romania cannot be a "market place". Its $13–14 billion imports represent the annual sale of a modest western company. However, the international financial bodies try to reduce those exports so that Romania stops looking around for money to finance the differences between imports and exports.

One can thus say that the programs of the international financial bodies might increase Romania's marginalization within the present world economic system, but nobody can say that they try to make Romania a "market place". In such a case, the IMF and the World Bank would have tried to promote economic development and not demolition, increase and not compression of the domestic demand or stimulation of exports. Unfortunately this is not the case of the Romanian economy.

PART II
THE MAIN PROBLEMS IN ECONOMY: APPROACHES AND RESULTS

CHAPTER 15

The sketch of the low inflation

Each administration in the post-December Romania – and almost each government within each administration – followed the same scenario in the attempt to accommodate their economic policy to the demands of IMF and of the World Bank, respectively. Therefore, each government at the beginning of its mandate invariably repeated two sketches that made up that scenario.

The former is the low inflation sketch. Under the IMF pressure, the governments planned a certain level of the annual inflation despite the fact that such a figure was impossible to reach. A low annual inflation could have been possible only if the wages in unproductive activities had not been paid in time or entirely. In other words, without refloating the country's economy neither inflation nor the fall of the *leu* exchange rate could be stopped. The so-called macro-stabilization – also asked by IMF – could not be thus established on a long term. On the other hand, an economic and social alternative must accompany economic refloating. The alternative can only be created by investments and there is no money for investments. Everybody is aware of that situation but nobody seems to care: neither the Romanian government nor the IMF. On the contrary, they are prepared to play the latter sketch: economic refloating with no money and privatization with no buyer. Almost ridiculously, precise time frames are decided for privatizations with no buyers or for closing down organizations in areas or sectors with no economic-social alternative. Mention should also be made that such time frames decided under pressure limit the ability to negotiate both the best price and post-privatization conditions.

Since the formulation "low inflation through economic refloating without money" cannot entail economic success, each government ended in doing its best or what it thought proper. Therefore, macro-stabilization has remained just a project.

At the beginning of their mandates, almost all the last four or five governments announced annual inflation rates of 20–25% or 30% the highest. As they were forced to finance the budgetary deficit, they launched on the market loans having a 20– 25% higher interest than the inflation rate in their declared intentions. The situation was rather ridiculous from the very beginning.

According to the government institution, the annual inflation rate had to be 25–30%; the annual rate of the interest offered by the very same institution for the public issue should have had about the same value or just a little higher. However, that was not the case. The difference was fabulous as compared to the forecast inflation rate. The only possible conclusion could be that either the government wanted to despoil its own budget by offering those interests or it did not believe in its own inflation prognosis.

Obviously, the latter variant is the correct one.

Such 25–30% inflations had been forecast for years although nobody believed in them and nobody considered them. The real values were in fact 40 –50%. It is almost a mystery that such a practice continued so long.

However, the mystery can be explained. The IMF – according to its cliché-ridden economic policy – does not agree with a country program that does not include a lower inflation than the previous year even if the experts realize that such a thing is practically impossible. That is the reason why despite the statistics that showed annual inflations of 40–50%, Romania absurdly promised only 25–30%.

In the present stage of the Romanian economy, an inflation of about 20–30% is impossible if the real sector of economy does not change dramatically. A cosmetic change in monetary economy cannot reduce inflation.
A big question mark remains however: could annual inflations of 20–25% be obtained on a medium term considering the difference between Romania's poor resources and the resources it needs to face the overwhelming problems it has to deal with?

Romania will never have the necessary resources – not even with a realistic foreign contribution – to solve its problems without destabilization. Inflation seems the easiest to cope with. The alternative is either massive unemployment (about 30% of the total workforce) or serious reduction of social security (to about a half).

The National Bank did its best to stop inflation. It even tried all kind of anti-economic measures: double interests as related to inflation rate; aberrant sterilization attempts to take *lei* out of circulation; minimal bank reserves of 20 or 30%, etc. Inflation could not be reduced to 25–30% but economy, in exchange, was severely affected for three consequent years.

Although some officials say that inflation is generated by profiteering, in fact the price hikes come from the production zone.

Utilities represent the main source of the price hikes (electricity, thermal energy, water and gas services, public transportation, etc.) because they are monopolies and they afford to transfer all their failures to the delivery prices, namely to their customers. The monopolist position practically excludes the concern to reduce costs and involves the possibility to increase prices in response to decreasing demand. Statistical data show unequivocally that price hikes in utilities field are by far the highest in economy

Between 1996 and 2000, when the IMF recipes were rather strictly applied, when the prices increased generally by 7.7% and the *leu* had a 7-time devaluation, the prices for electricity increased by 17 times, for thermal energy by 15 times, for natural gas by 24 times, for water by 13 times, for trains by 11 times, for public transportation by 12 times, etc. Obviously, such increases can only be reduced when utilities are no longer monopolies – a gradual and long-term action.

Therefore, the non-productive sector as a whole is the main source of inflation in Romania. As long as the expenses in that sector are not recovered and those working there get their entire wages in time, financing cannot be made from real sources but from inflation only.

CHAPTER 16

Anomalies in income policies

The income policy in Romania is inflationary since it is not built on an economic basis. The wage increases can represent only a part of the labor productivity growth and it should be correlated with the latter and not with the price increase that is a consequence of it. Obviously, the pension increases, entirely dependent on the wage increases, will follow the same pattern. Automatic indexations, with inflation rate of the wages in the budgetary system and in other sectors with State capital, and of pensions as well, mean promotion of inflation and a fake social security as the implicitly generated inflation will rapidly annul the initial effects of purchasing power growth.

Wages depend on labor productivity only. People say that prices in Romania are similar to those in Germany and the wages should be similar too. The genuine answer is that labor productivity in Romania is not similar to that in Germany either technically or organizationally. One should not be an economist to understand a simple fact: of the 4.4 million people working in the official economy in Romania, one million works in non-functional activities, namely in branches that are not able to recover the money they have spent. However, these people get their wages regularly, like the others, meaning that the latter support the former directly with their own wages, or indirectly, following inflation. The IMF demands that that people involved in non-functional activities should not be paid integral wages as they find it unacceptable that such wages are indirectly paid from the State budget on account of the budget arrears increase; on the other hand, the loss-generating organizations are not forced to pay either their debts or national insurances.

In 2000, instead of the usual stuff about closing down non-functional organizations, the program agreed upon by Isarescu government and IMF tried, for the first time, to reduce wages in loss organizations. After ten years of economic disorder and political abuse, the provisions included an equilibration of the wage compensation. For a decade, the wages of those who shouted louder were the only ones that could keep pace with the devastating inflation. The most favored were however those working in monopolist organizations who blackmailed politically and socially. Anomalously, the organizations with the highest losses or with the highest debts were the ones with the highest wages as well. They had all monopolist positions in the market and their directors and trade unions did everything to their best advantage. On the other hand, the lowest wages were those in the ready-made, footwear, and forestry operation sectors, the very ones that kept the Romanian exports alive.

Had such provisions been applied, wages and performance would have been correlated for the first time in the State sector, with beneficial economic consequences. People should have no longer avoided the private sector as they do now, since a job in the State sector is not only surer but better paid as well.

An act of social injustice should have been at least partially corrected, since a government ordinance had stipulated that the managers of the State organizations could have wages 44 higher than the average wages in their organization. What about the spirit of the market economy? If the organization does not pay back the debts to its suppliers, creditors, and State budget it is no longer a market organization and its managers are not entitled to such high wages. Failure to pay the money they owe endangers the wages of those entitled to receive money from the budget and the fat wages in the organizations that cannot cover them mean to deprive other people who have no guilt at all.

No wage can be guaranteed without proper performance. In a market economy, a person working in a non-profitable organization cannot win better than someone working in an organization that covers its expenses and pays back its debts. To say nothing about the fat salaries of the managers in the former!

All these things could have been solved long ago, but they were not because of the politics and politicking. The pork-barrel politics was the main obstacle since the State enterprises were an important pipeline through which public funds were sucked away to the best interest of parties, groups, or private persons.

Practically, the political-trade-unionist schemes, aiming at preserving the tough nuclei of the State monopolies succeeded in turning into an empty notion the wage correlation with the situation of the organization accounts.

The government gave up in front of the trade unions pressure and the wage system in the non-profitable organizations went on following the same old rules.

Unfortunately, the government was the eternal loser in its battle with the trade unions. Isarescu government connected the wages in the organizations with arrears strictly to those arrears and started to reformulate economic laws. Performance-related pay, as an economic law, means to condition the wages by arrears, but also by increase in labor productivity, service quality, and, in non-profitable organizations, by restructuring measurements. The natural principle follows: a person in an organization having debts cannot win more than a person in an organization that pays all its debts in time. In fact, that was the very problem that had to be legally and administratively solved. The government remained thus unprotected in front of all the legal and administrative subterfuges the trade unions invoked.

Concretely, the government stipulated the following provision: no debts paid no remittance of the wage fund. More exactly, it is remitted within certain limits and the wages are not paid entirely. The bill of the 1997 budget included such a provision referring to the State-owned organizations and to their obligations, but the provision was not included in the budget law. A lot of reasons were invoked in the parliament debates. The wage funds were to be blocked by banks but the banks were not entitled to choose among the recipients of the customers' money orders. Even more important, the State did not have the legal right to preempt other unpaid creditors. On the other hand, bad payers might have had several bank accounts. Finally, yet importantly, the international conventions adopted by the International Labor Organization give priority to the wage rights. The trade unions used all these subterfuges while the government was not entitled to make the legal changes able to relate the respective debts with the payment of wages in the State organizations.

Nastase government failed in making such a correlation although they made a step forward and limited the wages of the managers in the State organizations, i.e. they could not exceed the wage of a State-secretary minister.

However, without a minimal investment program, able to create an economic alternative and to break the monopolist positions of several State organizations in the market, no government whatever could impose a correlation of wages with labor productivity, the first genuine sign of a reform.

The present structure of the Romanian economy does not allow inflation reduction without increase of the foreign deficit. Likewise, no serious attempt to restrain the deficit of the foreign current account could avoid inflation increase. The explanation is the resource-consuming machine without a corresponding economic effect represented by the loss-generating State enterprises.

A genuine policy for reducing inflation and foreign deficit must include reduction of activity in the non-functional economic sector. We like it or not, increase of unemployment rate is the only factor able to temperate inflation on a long term and to reduce the foreign deficit as a basis for a stable national currency.

Without a high unemployment rate, inflation in Romania will never reach one figure only. The generally accepted two-figure yearly inflation has to be atypically combined with a lower budgetary deficit (zero, if possible). Why atypical? Because inflation is generally the result of budgetary deficits. However, in Romania inflation could be the result of controlled economic monetization. Atypically, the State has to give up its position of funds borrower and leave the existing savings, few as they are, at the disposal of real economy that could thus recover. In this way, a more generous taxation base could be created for a budget that would become stronger and stronger.

By monetizing economy, inflation could be able to absorb the tensions in the system, the budget ones included. On the other hand, if the State were not so badly in debt, following decrease of the real interests, at least for a while, economy could finally start o develop.

CHAPTER 17

Macro-stabilization – an IMF project

The only responsible for macro-stabilization failure is the Romanian political class who did not implement reform; it did not even impose restructuring of the non-functional sector. Had the later been reduced, the impact on economy would have been less dramatic and macro-stabilization would have had another fate.

However, IMF had its guilt since its directions inspired and even guided economic policy in Romania.

17.1. "We agree, but go our own way"

During its first administration, PSDR followed the principle "*we agree, but go our own way*" in its relations with IMF. IMF says that the results were poor. On the other hand, PSDR say it was OK. The Peasant-Liberal-Democratic coalition followed the principle "*we agree and go their way.*" In fact, they did what they could because the largest part of the IMF demands could not be achieved. However, the results were poor, much poorer than during PSDR. Economy dropped and for a large majority of the Romanians the situation became simply dramatic. Ironically, IMF granted less financial credit and image credit implicitly, to the coalition than they had granted to the previous administration. Consequently, the 1996–2000 coalition was simply demolished and some if its members were completely sidelined.

Shortly, no post-December agreement with IMF was concluded and no government succeeded to take more than one credit installment. Of course, it was a vote of no confidence for the Romanian governments, irrespective of their color, but also a proof that the IMF recipes were not the best ones. They might as well have been a cause of failure.

The main goal of the IMF programs is the substantial reduction of inflation. For reaching it, the IMF asked severe restrictions in all the expenses components, mainly, let us say, the "visible" ones of the State. More exactly, the budgetary deficit has to be limited. Second, in the hidden expenses that are finally paid by the State as well; they are not included in the budget but are supported, immediately or on a long term, by it. Third, the restriction of the population expenses, the reduction of the population's consumption. Finally, the restriction of the investment expenses. Therefore, the global domestic demand must be reduced for hampering the price hikes. If inflation gets lower, it will induce – according to IMF – a relative stability of the national currency. The latter can also be obtained by decreasing the pressure in the currency market, as a compression of the domestic demand would discourage imports and consequently the hard currency demand.

Everything seems OK! IMF considers that a healthy economic increase can only be obtained when inflation has been significantly reduced and the national currency has become more stable. However, IMF does not show the way to be followed for such an increase. IMF offers recipes for economic restriction and not for economic increase!

What actually happens? The restriction wave breaks over the most vulnerable area – investments – and avoids the current survival expenses. In this way, no new resources are created and this means a real disaster on a long term. A vicious circle thus appears: next year the resource restrictions are even more dramatic.

The State budget itself starts its restrictions with capital expenses. That is why the Romanian budget has long ceased to be a development factor and has turned into a simple survival tool.

On the other side, the non-functional sector, the area where the most resources are wasted, is the most restrictions-proof. The resource restriction is more complicated there since the resources allowance is indirect. Loss-generating organizations practically survive due to the indirect subventions they receive: they are permitted not to pay their financial obligations mainly to the State budget and to the national insurance budget. Any further payment penalty means further non-payments and there is no other way than to close down those organizations. Easier said than done! Both socially and economically! As a mater of fact, they cannot be closed down without creating first some other economic alternatives which, in their turn, cannot be created without investments. And so on.

Therefore, the only one left to be restricted is the population's consumption: first, by relative reduction of the social allowances; second by the relative decrease of the pensions and wages. At this level, everything is in the hands of the political decision. If the officials ignore the population and do not pay their wages and pensions at all – as happened in Ukraine and Moldavia – inflation decreases and IMF has a good example to offer. If the government goes on paying wages and pensions, inflation cannot get lower, and IMF includes the example among the negative ones. This is the case of Romania.

Restriction for restriction's sake or non-payment of wages cannot be economic goals. A low inflation is practically useless if there is nothing left around it: no organizations, no people to work, no money to buy the goods that are finally no longer affected by inflation.

17.2. Recipes for an economic drop

Frustrated by PSDR slogan "we agree, but go our own way", IMF forced, in 1997, the new administration, still groping around, to achieve in seven months what IMF considered had not been achieved in seven years. Instead of asking the new Romanian government to finally privatize or wind up the loss-generating organizations, i.e. to start the structural reforms that had been avoided, IMF started to build up various monetary and budgetary programs with no chance of success as long as structural reforms remained as such. They asked for a liberalization of the exchange rate, transparency of the late subventions by including them into the budget, energy at its real cost, and doing away with the national production protection by dramatically decreasing customs duties for food and other imported goods. All these objectives were necessary and correct, but such an approach, considering a totally unprepared economy, proved both unrealistic and non-operational. Therefore, no goal was achieved.

The resources attracted by the economic organizations – the private ones included – were gradually turned into arrears and the largest part of them became public. The final creditor, the budget, overwhelmed by all these everlasting debts that would never be paid, entered a vicious circle that included economy as well.

As long ago as 1997, fall of the Gross Domestic Product, inflation, and the *leu* devaluation got out of control. Failure to keep inflation within reasonable limits pushed IMF to an unspeakable solution in order to limit the price explosion: they anchored the currency exchange rate. Consequently, the exports were so seriously discouraged and the imports so generously stimulated that the situation exceeded that in the Vacaroiu government, criticized by IMF itself for artificially girthing up the exchange rate. In 1998, the trade deficit reached the dramatic level of 40% of the export profit, as the external financing to support it was increasingly difficult to find.

Overwhelmed by the failure of its own recipe, IMF conceived the most embarrassing of all the possible programs for 1999. The goal – necessary and correct, by all means – was the reduction of the deficit of the external current account by at least $ 1 billion. The way of achieving such a goal was a draconic compression of the domestic demand by increasing taxes, decrease of the State expenses and limiting the budgetary deficit. Consequently, collapse in the population's consumption was supposed to reduce imports significantly. The imports reduced all right but they did not affect the resource waste in non-functional activities or the wealthy population; the only ones to suffer were the poor only. Compression of the internal demand through monetary measures or through "neuter" fiscal measures, i.e. nonselective, has no "neuter" effect whatsoever as it affects the poorer ones.

In fact, the strategy applied to reduce the external account deficit was much simpler. Romania was simply left alone and it had to do its best with no money at all, according to the principle "less external resources, less imports!" With this aim in view, all the procedure subterfuges were used. The decision-making instances of the Fund scheduled the discussion of the stand-by agreement in the latter half of the year, i.e. after the payment deadlines of the external debt. Further on, because of the almost embarrassing combination of new procedure subterfuges and new reproaches, the agreement was not signed until September. Finally, the first $70 million installment was delivered. The second higher installment was conditioned by contracting a $450-million loan from the international market of the private capital, within a non-operational experiment called "burden share" between IMF and the private capital in financing the slow-payer countries.

The very fact of forcing a poor country to borrow from the private capital is both defiant and disqualifying. More than that, to force it to accept a 20% interest for one-year long term only means that you are interested to destroy and not to help that country. More than that, IMF went on supporting the experiment even when the experiment proved to be a failure: the private capital refused to "share the burden" with IMF and finance Ecuador, leaving the country defaulted on the payment.

The year 1999 proved that Romania, despite the guaranty of its agreement with IMF, did not get either access to the international market of the private credit or an improvement of the country risk mark from the international rating agencies. More than that, the foreign investors simply avoided Romania because IMF invoked budgetary duress and, consequently, gave up all the facilities granted to investors.

Therefore, Romania concluded 1999 with about one billion less external debt than that it entered 1999, a situation reminding Ceausescu's expensive and counterproductive conceit. Was it necessary that a developing country drastically reduce its external debt?

Mention should also be made that in its relation with IMF, Romania is a net creditor, not a net debtor, i.e. the money it borrows from IMF is much less than its quota to the Fund.

17.3. A timely change

Three years of severe fall in economy following IMF programs, with no success in stopping inflation, required urgent change in economic policy. Isarescu government committed itself to do it. Contrary to the IMF recipes, Isarescu government tried to promote economic growth directly in the sphere of investments, before the calm down of inflation and stabilization of national currency.

The vicious circle was broken by fiscal relaxation that increased the self-financing rate of the economic organizations. Isarescu government initiated a fiscal relaxation for the economic organizations (by reducing the profit taxation rate from 38% to 25%) financed, out of budgetary reasons, by the population. VAT quota were "leveled off" at 19%, meaning that taxation was reduced for the physical "majority" of products and services and increased significantly for products and services having a prevailing financial weight (about 2/3) in the population's consumption (from 11% to 19% for some food products and from 0 to 19% for electric, thermal, and household energies). Such a taxation that brought bread and jewelry to the same level was somehow accepted by IFM, since it generalized neutrality of the public finances, thus meeting the IMF expectations. Therefore, Isarescu's program, beyond inversing the sequences in the IMF economic policy, treated more advantageously the taxation of the profits got from exports.

Based on that program a new agreement was concluded with IMF. Unlike the previous ones, the new agreement tried to identify solutions for such basic problems of real economy as: debts at the level of organizations within the field of public utilities and services or performance-related income policy. In fact, the new program left aside the priorities generally, but rather artificially agreed by IFM: control of inflation or of the currency exchange rate – derivatives that cannot be solved by monetary therapies at a macroeconomic level unless basic changes have taken place previously at a microeconomic level, i.e. within organizations.

Obviously, the solutions were far more complex than the classic recipes of controlling inflation and currency exchange rate by monetary means. Neither the Romanian government nor IMF had magic formulas for increasing economic output to say nothing of the financial discipline enforcement able to stop the repeated failures to pay the debts.

However, Isarescu government got a feeble economic recovery (important indeed since it came after three years of economic failure) and a serious expansion of exports.

17. 4. The key – small doses

In 2000, the new PSDR administration announced its recipes, taking into account a somewhat balance in economy. In fact, the recipes were not their own. They had already been applied in the West for several decades. It is true; they were given up about 15–20 years ago when the West entered a new development stage. However, they were extremely successful and the West owes its present prosperity to them. Therefore, they should not be given up altogether, since the stage of the transition economies is closer to that of the western ones 40–50 years ago.

According to those recipes, the key is the economic growth, i.e. investments and consumption. If a country lacks resources they have to be partly imported, and partly monetarily generated inside the country itself by the usual mechanisms of economic simulation. Therefore, a deficit of the external current account should be accompanied by a deficit in the State budget and by high inflation. All these should furnish, even if partly artificially, the necessary resources for increasing investments, the only ones able to create new genuine resources for the increase of the population's consumption as well. According to this conception, wages and pensions must increase above the economic possibilities, in order to stimulate demand.

To sum up, this conception envisages the demand stimulation for inducing economic growth. Once obtained, the latter would offer a basis for the absorption and gradual slowing down of inflation. One can easily notice the total contradiction existing between this approach and the IFM recipes that concentrate mainly on suffocating inflation by compressing demand, followed by economic increase.

According to the mentioned conception, Nastase government continued its election promises of social security and stimulation of economy (facilities for small and middle organizations, control of prices for energy, disguised subventions to unproductive State organizations, etc.). The only way to finance them was through budgetary deficit and mainly through external debt increase. Therefore, the incentive to consumption and investments increased the pace of the economic growth that had been already expected in the Romanian economy, at a lower level, of course. Unfortunately, very rapidly, in several months practically, the main balances in economy were affected: budgetary balance, external balance, the commercial one, and that of the checking account. Most dramatic, the economic growth was supported by an explosive increase of the arrears. Under such conditions, an agreement with IMF was practically impossible and as Nastase government could not afford a failure the initial exuberance faded away. Gradually, the smaller budgetary deficit and the cautious income policies – also asked for by IMF – made possible such an agreement. A new stand-by agreement was thus concluded between Nastase government and IMF in October 2001. In fact, Nastase government gradually gave away the initial recipes and changed its economic policy.

However, an alternative solution to IMF unsuccessful formulas does not mean to give up the fragile balance entailed by these formulas. It would mean simply to mock at the population who bore the burden; once the balance destroyed, it should be replaced by something else.

In order to ensure economic balance, by growth, not by restraint, the *key to success is to use small doses in simulating domestic demand.* Large doses compromise everything and this is mainly true in a country where financial discipline is nothing but a project yet.

External loans are not an alternative to the IMF programs: they could generate a hard-to-cover foreign deficit and a collapse menace to Romania.

Romania does need an alternative to IMF programs, but that should be serious and realistic, able to start building, slowly and soundly, without destroying the fragile balances got on expense of the millions of Romanians' sacrifices.

It is neither desirable nor possible to resume the economic policy of 1992–1996. The resources are fewer now and the possibilities to replace them less. Likewise, the government has no longer the support of the State banks, as many of them went bankrupt or were privatized.

It is however interesting to notice the change in the IMF point of view after PSDR started its new administration. In its negotiation with Romania, IMF somehow gave to the World Bank the role of a forerunner. Consequently, social adjustments agreed upon by the Romanian Government and the World Bank became premises for the macro-stabilization programs recommended by IMF, just the other way round than before. The institutions in Washington seem to have finally understood that, in the case of the Romanian economy (and maybe of other countries, as well), the monetary and budgetary programs are but useless exercises if they are not preceded, or accompanied at least, by real economy restructuring. Consequently, the financing got from the World Bank and the European Union would no longer be strictly conditioned by the green light offered by the macro-stabilization agreement concluded with IMF only. However, it is too late for the Romanian government: it either restructures the real economy, or it can no longer have any guaranty for external financing. Inflation and exchange rate do not lose their importance but become again what they really are: change derivatives in real economy and not illusory levers to entail such changes.

Nastase government is both the beneficiary and the one made responsible by the change in the attitude of international financial organizations. However, the change is beneficial to economy as long as it places in proper order the restructuring–macro-stabilization ratio.

CHAPTER 18

Arrears – more dangerous than inflation

As resources crisis was deeper and deeper, inflation became the safety valve for avoiding social and even economic explosions – a fact not entirely acknowledged, however. In this way, economy, the basis of which remained the same, kept moving each year to higher and higher price levels. If the deficit of external current account, i.e. net consumption of external resources, increases, inflation can be controlled. On the other hand, if consumption decreases Romania is forced to make net payments on credit from the external debt, as happened in 1999. In such a case, inflation can no longer decrease and it even re-inflames! If they try to stop inflation by constraining consumption and investments, two situations are likely to appear: either wages and pensions are not paid entirely or in time, or real economy creates, for its own survival, more artificial and more dangerous money than inflation itself: arrears, namely non-paid debts. Unfortunately, a vicious circle indeed!

Such unpaid debt – arrears – exists everywhere in the world. Unfortunately, it is explosive and already dangerous in Romania as it represents the equivalent of almost one half of the GDP. Nobody knows exactly what it can finally generate or how it can be stopped. In fact, it is not an external debt that could produce collapse if not paid in time; it is a kind of debt of the Romanian economy to itself, a kind of everybody's debt to everybody that increased gradually and seized almost all the economic organizations, private persons included.

Financially, this debt is called arrear as it is considered a delayed payment. Debt is a normal financial state. It is associated with credit, without which economy cannot work. Arrear is not a normal state because it represents a backlog, a debt that fell due but remained unpaid. An arrear generates another arrear and so on, an endless chain that buries in the State budget. All those involved in the payment blockage try to get out of it by not paying their debts to the budget, the only ones that are not a condition of the production. While a supplier could stop supplying, the State has no real coercion lever. The debt increases and delay penalties are just ignored, similarly to the initial arrears. The budget arrears should be given a different name in Romania since they are not delay payments, but debts that will never be paid. Such arrears that will never be paid are possible in Romania where legislation favors debtors and not creditors as usual. Since the debts are not paid, the State budget enters the same vicious circle and it does no longer do its normal duties, being late in paying wages, reducing the allocations for health, education, culture, public order, and national defense.

18.1. "Financial blockage" diversion

Financial blockage is, in fact, an accumulation of arrears in the whole economy. The term is a diversion since the phenomenon is officially presented as a kind of misfortune with no one responsible for it, a by-product of transition, or, even worse, of reform itself. Under such formulas, they try to hide the real state of things: it is a transfer instrument of financial resources from population and for profitable activities to the unprofitable ones. Economic organizations blame the "financial blockage" for the disaster they produced, ever mentioning how much they have to receive but systematically forgetting to mention their debts.

The "financial blockage" is an intentional mess of payments or, more exactly, an intentional acceptance of irredeemable debts among State organizations. Concretely: the State organizations were free to contract debts – supplies from other State organizations or loans from State banks – although it was pretty sure that they would never have money to pay them back. State debtors are never asked letters of credit from the bank when they order something, no bank ever forecloses on them or does it for the sake of appearance only. In fact, the State organizations fall practically outside the bankruptcy law jurisdiction.

However, the Romanian government and IMF started to consider the arrears accumulated in economy a basic problem and to look for solutions in 2000 only. The Romanian governments tried to avoid direct approach of this topic and to postpone it to a distant future instead of asking the IMF experts' assistance. Such a position was adopted because the so-called "financial blockage" – i.e. the arrears chain – was the way of keeping "alive" the great debtors. At the same time, IMF did not pay due attention to the arrears problem. Even worse, they thought that the restraints they recommended for reducing inflation and stabilizing national currency would finally reduce arrears as well. Unfortunately, it did not happen that way!

Quite the opposite! It was the IMF program that increased the arrears – directly by severely reducing the domestic demand and indirectly by reducing GDP – to the end of the 1990s, following their demand to reduce concomitantly the budgetary deficit and the quasi-fiscal one (use of public funds for State structures that do not appear in the budget directly), and mainly to reduce drastically the deficit of external current account (net consumption of external resources).

Payment constraints that increased fabulously were followed, in response, by a fabulous fail to pay the debts. The resources attracted by the economic organizations, the private ones included, gradually turned from debts into stale debts:

they became arrears. Arrears increased as a whole from 36.3% GDP equivalent in 1996 to about 45% GDP equivalent in 2000. The own capital/debts ratio was 1.4 in 1996 but dropped to 0.6 in 2000. Therefore, the liability call increased more than two times and became more important than the recourse to the own capital in the activity of the economic organizations. In order to face constraints, the economic organizations turned almost 38% debts into arrears, in comparison with 32% in 1996. The public budgets gathered 22% of the stale debts total (in comparison with 19%) and they practically took over the decrease of the arrears towards banks that stopped crediting the real economy. The last creditor, i.e. the State budget, became so overwhelmed by debts that it could no longer be the engine in economy.

Therefore, without previous or at least concomitant economic measures rooted in real economy, the latter will respond to any budgetary and monetary constraints by increasing arrears. They are the last money the real economy could benefit from – artificial money, more dangerous and harmful than the inflation money itself.

18.2. Contamination of private persons

The increasing poverty of the population generated even more debts to public utilities. More often than not, the electric bills were higher than the incomes of many families. Therefore, arrears, i.e. financial blockage, contaminated private persons as well.

The excessive increase in the public utility tariffs (the very result of transferring monopolistic suppliers' problems to consumers) gradually reduced the population's consumption. No matter how much tariffs increase from now on, population cannot pay more and public monopolies cannot expect more money from the population. The population's consumption will be lower and lower, although Romania is already on the verge. Public utility monopolies will have to change between sacrificing social peace and accepting even more arrears from organizations and from population as well.

Obviously, under such circumstances, increase of arrears is expected. However, IMF insists that the Romanian government should reduce them, although the results are uncertain and they might not be realistic altogether. The economic data show that neither economic organizations nor population can pay more than they already do, and any further constraint turns into an arrear. Therefore, rapid and important reduction of arrears is a mere illusion. Waiving the so-called "historical debts" – mainly delay increments and penalties – for certain economic organizations, as a kind of gift from the State, is a fake that encourages good payers to become bad payers. The only solution is a long-term one: an operational bankruptcy institution accompanied by genuine economic development could gradually increase the economic payment capacity. Otherwise, the vicious circle will persist.

18.3. The Gordian knot of the exploitation losses

Surprisingly, 45% of the money blocked at the end of the 1990s came from the private sector. That situation appeared in 1995 and practically accompanied the development of the mentioned sector from then on. Unfortunately, the conclusion is devastating: neither the private sector in Romania nor privatization can be solutions for the deep-rooted damage in economy.

"Financial blockage" statistics include the category "mixed property," meaning organizations with a majority of State capital and private shares following the mass privatization program. Obviously, such mixed property is nominal and it should be included in "State property" category (made up of monopolies, autonomous (State) companies and State trading companies). However, it is interesting sometimes to compare the financial results: the mixed-property organizations are by far the worst.

The huge weight of the private sector within the "financial blockage" total requires more careful analysis.

Statistically, in 1999–2000, the private sector contributed 62% to GDP but it included mainly branches with little capital and little equipment (trade, services, and subsistence agriculture). The private sector weight within the total social capital is ridiculous as well: less than 1/3. In industry, the main important branch in economy, the private sector weight (both in turnover rate and in social capital) is simply marginal.

The general lack of capital is even higher in the private sector. The financing funds are very few; their slightly higher weight in the own capital of the private economic organizations is only due those organizations miniature social capital (hundreds of private economic organizations had practically social capitals of 100 000 *lei* until 1998, when social capital compulsorily increased to 2 000 000 *lei*, a small amount as well). Consequently, the private sector can only work by massively attracting resources that are sometimes 4–5 times higher than the social capital of the respective organizations. Objectively, in each moment, at a low rate of own capitalization they have to rely on extended debts (from banks, suppliers, budget, etc.). Such debts have to exist as a working condition until an increase of the own capitalization rate has been achieved.

The conclusion is rather obvious: the State sector is still the deciding factor in economy, and mainly in industry as an overwhelming impact branch that monopolizes the public utilities and the main supplies. The private sector has not reached the "critical mass" yet to decisively influence or dictate the market rules in economy. More than that, it is partly parasitical and has no interest whatsoever in eliminating the State sector, without which its survival in a competition world would be much more difficult. Therefore, the private sector is infected by the State sector and copies its behavior deliberately, since the succeeding governments keep favoring the latter. There is no wonder then that the private economic organizations keep postponing, in their turn, to pay their debts to other private economic organizations, and mainly to the State ones.

However, the private sector is not a worse payer than the State one; it is the only one left that still has some profitable activities. More than 3/4 of the official economy net profit came from the private sector. Unfortunately, following the constraints in the last years of the previous decade, the net losses in the private sector increased spectacularly and represented 44% of the total net losses in official economy. However, although the private sector was forced to increase the gearing, its arrears got lower (27% in 1999 and 31% in 1996). At least it pays a part of its debt in time. Therefore, the private sector is a better payer than the State one that never pays back its duties: more than 45% of its debt has become arrears (compared with 35% in 1996).

Statistics show that while the debts to suppliers have practically the same weight, the quota of the debts to banks decreased dramatically, as the banks draconically reduced the credits to real economy. The public budgets, that close the circle, took over the burden.

Practically, no economic segment was able to take over the shock of the ample changes in economic policies at the beginning of 1997: transparency of hidden subsidies, refuse to deliver electric and thermal energy under real costs, no artificial support of the currency exchange rate, considerable limitation of budgetary and quasi-fiscal deficit, liberalization of foreign trade by massive reduction of customs tariffs.

Concretely, varied economic segments responded by trying to escape constraints how they could.

The State sector responded to the banks lack of involvement in real economy by simply overwhelming the budget: its quota of debts to budget almost doubled and represented more than half of the total. More exactly, the State sector did not pay its taxes and thus used the fiscal credit and turned an important part of its budgetary obligations into arrears.

The private sector used the trade credit and increased its debts to suppliers. During the same interval, its debts to suppliers represented half of the total. The private sector cannot afford great debts to the State budget; they represent less than 10% of its arrears.

The situation of the so-called "mixed property" is however intolerable: more than 57% of its debts are backlog, in comparison with 32% in 1996. Nobody should wonder since these State-capital organizations have no owner. The managerial staff has no responsibility whatsoever and they have nobody to give an account to. The mass privatization that changed the structure of their capital was mere mockery that diluted the owner's authority and loosened management. Finally, yet importantly, mention should be made of the bad influence generated by the promises of waiving and deferring debts before privatization. Between 1996 and 1999, the net losses of those organizations increased dramatically, about 3.6 times; their gearing dependence increased 3.8 times; and their backlogs were 6.7 times higher. The financial situation of these organizations – theoretically ready to be privatized – is dramatic. The account books show that even if they cashed up all their debts their total payment capacity would not exceed 40% of the global quantum of their debts.

The State sector is a worse payer than the private one because its exploitation losses are higher: 50% in the State sector vs. less than 20% in the private one. These quotas are almost self-evident since the exploitation losses, i.e. those in the current activity, are the starting point of the backlogs that start a genuine chain reaction afterwards. These very losses generate the "financial blockage" through their insolvency. However, to blame the "financial blockage" when an organization has exploitation losses is pure diversion.

Obviously, Romania will only be able to get free from the vicious circle of the "financial blockage" if its very nucleus, i.e. losses, is attacked. Stronger budgetary and monetary constraints should combine with due bankruptcy processes so that economic organizations generating losses could be get rid of.

CHAPTER 19

"Debts equity swap" – a worth trying scheme

According to certain opinions, converting debts into shares could reduce arrears. The schemes called "debt equity swaps" are largely used in market economies and they are operative and effective when those involved in them are ownership rights holders. However, in Romania they wanted to use these schemes for debts that the State has to cash up from State-owned organizations.

According to the agreed regulations, the State is authorized to sell the debts it has to receive from State-capital organizations; in exchange for the debts taken over, the buyer could get shares in the respective organizations. The State-owned shares in those organizations pass from the representative of the employer-State (now APAPS, ex FPS – The Management of State-owned Property) to the Ministry of Finance (as a representative of the public authority-State) and the latter would thus become both debtor and creditor. In fact, such an action is intended to recover partly the debts of the State organizations the privatization of which could thus be stimulated.

Supporters of "debt equity swap" emphasize the success of the scheme in several South American countries, among which Argentina and Chile. There are however some aspects that make the Romanian case distinct. Those countries applied the scheme to liquidate a part of their external debts in order to avoid being defaulted on the payment. Foreign creditors themselves were deeply interested since they could thus get back part of their money.

The situation in Romania is quite different: they try to pay domestic debts with foreign money.

To stimulate the involvement of foreign money, the South-American countries offered massive share packages in potentially profitable companies. In Romania, such a scheme would only solve the problems of non-profitable or even bankrupt companies.

If the companies are profitable or if they could become profitable, the shares will be easily taken over. There will always be capital market speculators ready to risk buying at a lower price if real chances of serious earnings exist. On the other hand, the common capital market speculators avoid companies with great losses and arrears; the potential buyer has to be a direct investor in the activity field of the respective organization, the only one able to appraise the chances of rehabilitation.

Therefore, in the case of non-profitable companies an indirect route is taken to reach the same point of direct privatization to strategic investors.

On a whole, the problems are the same and, consequently, the chances are about the same. However, the "debt equity swap" scheme is worth trying. If the State sells its debts and if the action is properly prepared, the legal and economic complications are fewer than if the State waives or reschedules its debtors' debts, a fact that could encourage good payers to become bad payers. Likewise, the chances of conversion operation will be higher if no rigid prices exist. The discount is the very essence of "debt equity swamp" mechanism.

The use of the scheme in privatizing Sidex-Galati – converting into shares a massive part of the aggregate works "historical" debts and taking over shares with a substantial discount by the private owner – is an important precedent for the possible privatization of the "black holes" existing in economy.

In such circumstances, the IMF opposition to using the scheme seems rather strange, since the private beneficiaries of some foreign credits got by the Romanian State warranty do not pay and the Romanian State itself has to pay for them. Unfortunately, this is one of the classical cases of the post-December privatization of profits and nationalization of losses, falsely called either capitalism or "market economy". However, IMF was against the Romanian State taking over some of the debtor's shares in exchange for their debts and organizing takeover bids for them. IMF pretended it was nationalization, but it was not. Simply, it was taking shares from private organizations without money and giving them to private organizations with money or from those who disregard the Romanian State to those ready to respect the Romanian State. Anyhow, IMF proved to be the defender of other interests than those of the market economy. If the interests defended by IMF are foreign, that means IMF promoted a kind of "externalization" of profits and an "internationalization" of losses. Free repatriation of business profits obeys the market economy rules when profits got by market activities are involved (not some earnings got by the pork-barrel politics on account of the Romanian State).

CHAPTER 20

Restructuring – a reform Cinderella

Restructuring need in the Romanian economy is beyond discussion. Restructuring is the very essence of reform: it represents reform at a microeconomic level, i.e. at the basis of economy. Any reform at macroeconomic level risks to be compromised if not accompanied and supported by restructuring. Unfortunately, this is the case of the Romanian economy, where market economy institutions are frail and the rules of market economy pure theoretical; the macro-stabilization attempts disappear one after another because no important step has been made in restructuring.

Restructuring means efficient reallocation of resources. That means that restructuring should give up production without market and production with losses because they represent waste of resources. Restructuring means also closing down loss-generating organizations that cannot pay their debts and thus make up the nucleus of the vicious circle of the arrears blocking economy. The resources should be thus directed to market activities having good chances of profit.

The privatization role in this process of resource reallocation is self-obvious. Logically, private property relies on profit, on moving resources from inefficient to efficient activities, and on giving up if these goals fail. Therefore, privatization means efficient economic activities and not wastes of public funds in inefficient activities. That is why privatization is an important part of restructuring.

20.1. Demolition and reconstruction at the same time

Obviously, restructuring is a dichotomous process: it means demolition and reconstruction alike. Non-profitable or without market activities are not abandoned for demolition's sake only; competitive and profitable activities should be built instead.

These restructuring generals show exactly the drawbacks of the post-December officials' action. Consequently, restructuring is the great absentee in the Romanian transition.

During the first Iliescu administrations, in an unrealistic attempt to keep the entire industrial "dowry," some survival injections were tried with no result whatsoever.

The Peasant-Liberal-Democratic coalition observed the IMF and the World Bank approach. The programs of these organizations insisted on the demolition side of restructuring and paid no attention to the construction one. However, experience demonstrated that the correct objective of liquidating unprofitable organizations could not be met without constructing something instead. The government, whatever its color, avoids liquidations and the organizations accumulate even more debts. Restructuring thus becomes more expensive and privatization more unlikely.

Restructuring, a both permanent and general process, is the responsibility of the economic organizations. However, in Romania, the ex-centralization of resources allocation, their scarcity, and the restructuring amplitude required a national strategy. Despite the possible danger hidden behind such a formulation (it could disguise an extension of the harmful centralism), a punctual appraisal of chances, a draft of possible scenarios, and the choice of the most advantageous variant were necessary. However, an industrial policy was absent, namely a policy able to concentrate domestic resources and to attract the foreign ones towards activities with the best chances on foreign markets.

A somehow tragic continuity existed in Romania. Ceausescu replaced the objective analysis of resources and possibilities with his own wishes: he created an industry intended to do everything and, naturally, he succeeded in creating one able to do nothing. He wasted huge resources and a large part of the industry he created went on wasting resources.

Iliescu administration lacked any industrial strategy and struggled to preserve the existing industrial model, despite the fact that it was outdated and expensive. He did not even try to change it formally.

The RDC-DP administration went on without an industrial policy: they openly asserted that they promoted a strict neutrality of public finance towards the industrial sectors. With such words picked up from the stock of theoretical liberalism, the coalition refused itself the right of concluding a concentration of the national efforts and of allocating the resources towards sectors and activities having better chances. That is the very essence of industrial policy! A policy using market economy instruments: fiscal facilities, credit facilities, customs facilities. All "liberal" countries use such facilities; all of them have an industrial policy. All of them try – through more or less orthodox methods – to protect themselves against an increasingly aggressive foreign competition and – using the same methods – to support the competitiveness of their products on the international markets. Ignoring the principle of public finance neutrality, the great liberal powers built their present industrial bases that help them face the harsh international competition, i.e. the competition existing among them.

20.2. No priorities, no choices

Neutrality of public finance could be the aim of a grown up market economy, in no case of Romania's. On the other hand, it compromises the chances of adopting a "crenellated" structure of industrial activity: a narrower range having some competitive "peaks" on foreign markets. Small countries found such niches and they manage among the market segments occupied by the great powers of the business world.

Unfortunately, the obscure market forces could not remove the monopolies that control the resource allocation in Romania. Nobody could ever remove them without an administrative intervention of the State, following the market signal, of course.

Without any priority and without a proper policy, everything turned into an extremely expensive improvisation. In an economy with no market, they left market to decide. Therefore, market decided that there were no longer competitive advantages in any field, and the few advantages existing at the beginning of transition were gone. The great "opportunities" discovered by the market forces in the Romanian economy are beer and mineral water bottling and raw wood exploitation by destroying forests.

With no attempt to choose among several variants, restructuring rapidly turned into an object of intention political campaigns followed by long interpolations of lack of action. Taking into account the impact of the loss-generating big State organizations at the general economic level, any political intention focused on such organizations. They remained practically the same and nothing was done for the general restructuring either. More exactly, the losers swallowed the resources and blocked restructuring of the healthy part of economy, thus narrowing any restructuring possibility of the non-profitable sector itself.

20.3. Liquidations – where and why?

There are more than 2100 loss-generating and in-debt organizations in Romania and 150 of them are responsible for more than 90% of the whole prejudices, meaning that budget, inflation, currency, imports, exports, and foreign payments form a vicious circle.

These organizations offer products or services in exchange for which they do not obtain, *no matter the reason*, returns that could cover their expenses. *No mater the reason!* The reasons may be diverse – some of them entirely transparent (lack of order, stocks), some others hidden (high artificial costs, monopoly prices), and quite a lot purposely distorted (blaming of the "financial blockage": they have to receive money, but have to pay their debts as well). These organizations can have higher expenses than profits because they are allowed not to pay the money they owe to their suppliers (mainly to raw materials and power suppliers, to banks, State budget and the budget of national insurance). The great losers are usually those having no option or those that do not have retort means or are not allowed to use them. For instance, the national electricity company takes the liberty not to pay its coal supplier because it is the only customer of the latter (that offers it a very poor product, anyway). The great industrial consumers take the liberty not to pay for the electricity because the electricity company is not allowed to stop supplying the State organizations. Finally, the State organizations take the liberty not to pay to the State budget and to the budget of national insurance because they know that the State cannot declare them bankrupt.

The vicious circle is obvious and it can be broken in three ways only.

The first is generally called "restructuring." Restructuring is expensive because it means reorganization, rightsizing, or redirection to the needs of the market, but also updating or even partial or total change in the line of business. As Romania has no money and as everything comes to money, only cosmetic changes are made that succeed in wasting the few funds allotted. The experiment made during Iliescu administration, mainly during Vacaroiu government, is a good example. Leaving aside the ideological, political, social, or electoral motivations connected with that uninspired experiment, its failure is explained by lack of money. The teams of Iliescu administrations did not understand that Romania did not have and would never have enough money to restructure its whole industry. At that time, the only solution was to leave aside parts of the industrial sectors in order to save the rest of them. Consequently, nothing was restructured and the whole industry suffered decline and higher difficulties.

The second way is privatization; restructuring is left in the hands of the new owners. Unfortunately, nobody considered it seriously in the case of the in-trouble organizations. Iliescu administrations in the first seven years following December 1989 rejected the idea: they would have had to accept very low-priced privatizations. The coalition that took power in 1996 absurdly struggled to demonstrate that, unlike their predecessors, they would embark on privatization. Unfortunately, they concentrated on profitable (easy to sell) organizations and left aside those having losses or debts that should have been a priority.

In this way, closing down loss-generating factories remains the only solution left. In closing down these organizations, the main criterion is the loss level/wages ratio. If the losses are lower than the wages amount, closing down the factory is not an emergency. Obviously, the wages are considered social spending, at least at the beginning of the liquidation process of the losses in economy.

In many organizations however, the amount of the unpaid debts exceeded the amount of the money paid for wages. In such cases, closing down is a must since the workplace costs more than it can produce, and keeping it does no longer mean social spending since it wastes resources (energy, raw materials, equipments). Therefore, closing down such factories is more profitable both for economy and society, even if the redundant staff is paid the equivalent wages. The only exception could be made in the case of a factory in a mono-industrial area, where alternative measures are compulsorily.

Loss-generating organizations are not a new phenomenon and, but for a few exceptions in mining, no post-December government has dealt with the problem directly yet. Why?

Obviously, the main motivations are economic. Loss-generating organizations are not isolated; they are part of an industrial chain and more often than not have important positions. A lot of them are in mono-industrial areas, and towns or even larger areas depend on them. Finally, exports come mainly from these loss-generating factories. All these problems were known when the Romanian economy started to get itself free, and to follow the market economy principles. In 1990, when the Romanian foreign trade ceased to be a State monopoly, such loss-generating organizations could no longer resist, especially when one of their main markets, COMECOM, disappeared. They could not resist the foreign competition and to maintain them was increasingly expensive.

If all these data had been taken into account and such organizations had been given up, technical and economic solutions could have been found and the process itself would have been less painful, both economically and socially.

Unfortunately, the direction followed was different; the increasingly complicated problems and the increased social cost required abrupt action. A higher economic and social price had to be paid because the action did not start when it had to because of both objective and subjective reasons: ideological, political, and electoral.

20.4. From ideological to economic reasons

The ideological reason was predominant immediately following 1989. Petre Roman government that started reform with half measures and expensive populisms did not intend to make real economy healthier and therefore did not even touch bankrupt factories. Nor did Stolojan, Roman's successor. Stolojan government succeeded in setting into some kind of order an economy turned by the previous NSF management into chaos. At the same time, they made a step backward in solving the crucial problem of the loss-generating organizations: they initiated the greatest debts waive of the mentioned organizations, in a wrong attempt that a fresh start would be made from "zero." Therefore, such organizations got the wrong impression that they could go on contracting debts that would never have to be paid back.

The NSF ideological principle – all factories represent people's work and they have to be preserved, obsolete and useless as they are – was the Iliescu administration's line of conduct.

A strictly political reason backed up the ideological one: no loss-generating organization should be closed down. Protected against any change, all the managers in such organizations turned into clients of Iliescu administrations, and the so-called “working class” in the State monopolist organizations (autonomous or trading companies) became the main segment of these administrations electorate.

A system of hidden subventions was schemed to avoid unemployment in these organizations. However, the subventions had to be covered: the solution found was inflation through forcing expenditures above the people’s own incomes and foreign credits. Therefore, the population paid indirectly by inflation and then directly since the consumption in absolute terms decreased.

Consumption decreased first in 1997: the domestic resources dried up and the need appeared to keep a balance between State’s expenses and incomes. The second decrease was required in 1999 when some balance had to be maintained in foreign accounts as well.

The situation was roughly the same during RDC-DP administration: none of the governing political forces following 1996 included in its program sanitation measures for real economy. However, other forces rose against such measures. As soon as someone tried to close down bankrupt organizations or just to stop the anti-economic expenses of supporting them with public funds, somebody else tried to block someway the action: trade-unions, “spontaneous” rioters who stopped traffic, politicians who backed up, directly or not, such actions.

Last but not least, in Romania nobody closed down a factory. Ever! Therefore, nobody knew exactly what to do in such a case. It was not just closing the gates. Obviously, closing up a factory is rather similar to opening a factory: it cost money. The only companies genuinely closed down in Romania were pigs or chickens combines left without subventions. They were thus forced to cease their activities;

what was left behind after closing the gates was stolen. The liquidation was thus complete. Paperless liquidation, yet liquidation.

CHAPTER 21

Amortizations and reform

The fear to radically change the amortization regulations, mainly in conditions of inflation that required major reconsideration, could explain the degradation in the Romanian economy and the lack of restructuring as well.

Any act of production involves workforce that uses, on the one hand, raw materials that are entirely included in the new product, and, on the other hand, equipments that are used in several production cycles and partly transfer their value to the new product. Therefore, recovering expenditures made for getting raw materials is different from recovering expenditures made for equipments. In the former case, expenditures are recovered by including them in costs at once, whereas in the latter they are included in costs gradually, with the wear and tear of the respective equipment in a production cycle.

To recover expenditures is a problem of life and death for economy. The quotas or installments – also called amortizations – are included into costs but, at the same time, the amounts recovered in the amortization accounts by selling products are gathered in a special fund – of amortization – and can be used for replacing the obsolete equipments. Therefore, the sooner the recovering the higher the possibility to renew equipments will be – a crucial thing in technical progress.

The retrograde conception during the Romanian communism was that low amortization quotas should be promoted in order to have low costs. Equipments devised to last 10–15 years, for example, had to be amortized in 30 years. At the same time, technically developed countries promoted rapid amortization and could thus recover rapidly in costs the equipment wear and tear. Therefore, Romania had a mediocre progress rate, while the other countries had very high ones.

The communist approach continued after 1989, with a new element: inflation increased deterioration. The galloping inflation abruptly reduced the amortization funds because the equipments inventory value was in *lei* that kept devaluing. In five years, one million *lei* recovered for a car was practically enough to buy a... wheelbarrow. Impossibility to speed up recovering through accelerated amortizations weakened the poor amortization investments. Astonishingly, Vacaroiu government adopted a regulation according to which the State organizations used to stop recovering in costs the amortization of equipments corresponding to the unused production capacity. De-capitalization was thus complete. Finally, the regulation favoring the economic organizations with much equipment and little production was abrogated.

Concretely, the economic organizations should be allowed, first, to bring the value of their production equipments up to date in order to avoid de-capitalization, and second, to recover rapidly the equipment expenditures in order to increase amortization investments and the chance of renewal. The former possibility is controversial and generates multiple adverse effects. The latter is connected with a new budgetary philosophy because the State should accept reduction of some receipts from profit taxes for stimulating economic organizations to invest in technological renewals. Recovery of the amortization quotas in costs means to consider them deducible expenditures, after subtracting the profit to be taxed.

Although a modern system for calculating profit was introduced in 1995, the regulations of the accelerated amortizations remained the same.

IMF's position was unhappy and rather retrograde: they insisted, out of budgetary reasons, on giving up the natural norms of economic operation, set up in 1997 by an emergency ordinance concerning direct investments that permitted economic organizations to use accelerated amortizations without the approval of the Ministry of Finance. Fortunately, Nastase government re-enacted this possibility in 2001 as part of the regulations concerning stimulation of direct investments higher than $1 million. However, a counterproductive discrimination was made: the same equipment might be subject to amortization regime if it belongs to an investment higher than $1 million or might not if its owner has less money.

CHAPTER 22

State companies: Who is their owner? Who makes the decisions? Who manages them?

One of the major obstacles to restructuring the State-capital factories is the ambiguity existing in their articles of association and in their relations with the economic environment. Nobody knew exactly in Romania who was the owner of those organizations (more exactly who represented the owner-State), who made the decisions and who managed them, or what the roles of their creditors were.

When Victor Ciorbea was a prime minister, he declared that neither the government nor SPF closed down factories, but market economy. Behind these words, Ciorbea government tried in fact to exonerate the government from the political burden of such a decision, and blamed the "market economy" for everything. In reality, the Prime Minister's words disclosed the institutional deadlock reached, very difficult, or even impossible to break.

At the beginning of the 1990s, the State organizations to be privatized became autonomous. Unfortunately, autonomous management was mistaken for dereliction of owner's authority, so that no one knows now who the owner of these organizations might be. Taking advantage of the absence of a legal owner, losses and debts accumulated. During NSF governments, Iliescu and Roman set up SPF's (State Property Funds) and PPF's (Private Property Funds), genuine inventions to increase and perpetuate confusion.

However, the only certain thing is that the owner is not the government and therefore the government cannot close down those loss-generation organizations. In a market economy this would be the creditors' or the owner's role. In Romania, the creditors and the bad-payers are the State. The only one left would be thus the owner. Legally, the representative of the owner-State (SPF changed into APMSP – Authority for Privatization and Management of State Participations) is not the owner, but a stockholder, not directly affected by the losses of its organizations. Who pays for these losses? Is it SPF (APMSP)? No, the population. However, SPF or APMSP does not care about population.

22.1. Owner-State – a harmful uncertainty

Therefore, as the government does not represent the owner-State but the public authority, the owner-State is practically represented by no one.
SPF that received 70% of the capital when the organizations were turned into "trading companies" was to be the representative of the owner-State. However, SPF took advantage of the lack of clear stipulations and tried to make a distinction between its qualities of a majority stockholder and of an owner. Thus, it played either the role of the stockeholder (and it did not make decisions) or of the owner (and it made decisions) as a function of its interests. More and more confusion was thus spread.

Nastase government turned SPF into APMSP and placed it within the jurisdiction of the executive power, solving only partly the legal and institutional problems of the State organizations to be privatized. Officially, the government is indirectly made responsible for those organizations; legally, the government as an institution is not a stockholder in them. Thus, decisions on privatizations and liquidations can no longer be passed on between the executive and APMSP – an important step indeed. However, the crucial problem "who is to respond for losses and unpaid debts" is still unsolved.

More than that, the program of mass privatization seems to have complicated the things even more. In many organizations, the population has taken over more than 30% of the freely distributed quotas of their capital; there are cases in which almost 60% has been taken. Obviously, the new majority is highly spread and the ownership so diffuse that the stockholders representing it have no word to say. Therefore, there is no possibility of reaching a major decision on the fate of the respective organizations. The small and numerous stockholders may legally contest any decision and any contestation blocks privatization and liquidation. As nobody is made responsible for losses, the population has to pay for them. The program of mass privatization is an important step forward, but in the specific situation in Romania everything has become even more complicated: who is the one to decide in these organizations?

Anytime the associative type private property (shares, with disseminate portfolio) comes from State property, and not from individual private property, the perverse effects of the confused relations existing among stockholders–board of directors–managers appear.

The direct consequences of such a situation are the decisional abuses of the managers who behave as if those organizations were their properties, and the restructuring blockage, mainly when the people working there are stockholders as well. The case of the organizations privatized by the hybrid MEBO method is highly significant.

Without properly denying the advantages of the MEBO method, mention should be made that the managers' authorities in the organizations privatized by that method suffered because of the dual status of those working there: stockholders and employees at the same time, a confusing status for most of them.

The same confusion governs the external relations of the MEBO privatized organizations. They are largely indebted to their ex-owner. If the market economy laws worked, the creditor would have to get assets from the organization capital in exchange for the debts that would never be paid. However, in this way, the respective organization would be nationalized again, and so on.

Finally, yet importantly, the so-called corporate governance is no properly regulated in Romania.

22.2. The hide-and-seek game of bankruptcy

If market economy in Romania had reached the basis of real economy thousands of State organizations would have long been closed down or sold.
However, the international financial institutions themselves got involved in the mockery market economy that closed down organizations in Romania and asked from the governments in Bucharest lists and the exact names of the organizations to be closed down. Why did they not leave market economy do that? Because there is no proper market economy able to trigger such a mechanism. The only one able to close down such organizations is the government and nothing else. It is not in the spirit of market economy but it is the only solution. Market economy will never be able to get rid of the burden of loss-generating factories.

No proper law of bankruptcy operates in Romania. Obviously, the lowest basis of such a law is a rather general legal norm stipulating foreclosure by order. Such a norm existed in Romania but it was practically abolished during communism, when the State was the only owner.

Unfortunately, the very absence of that legal norm encouraged free will in allocation of resources and in wasting them.

In Romania, foreclosure by order is the missing pillar and its absence turned bankruptcy into a frail and non-functional institution.

When IMF forced Vacaroiu government to promote a bankruptcy law, they produced something so complicated and knotty that avoided the very term "bankruptcy" and used "financial insolvency" instead. Practically, no State organization, not even a broken one can be declared "bankrupt," and the legal procedures are so complicated and time consuming that liquidation becomes impossible.

During 1996–2000, the liberal staff at the Ministry of Justice considered that "embezzled bankruptcy" is an act or practice with no object whatsoever since "bankruptcy" was replaced by other terms and it should be therefore given up. Following media intervention, both terms were re-legislated.

Fortunately, the 1996–2000 administration introduced the possibility of appeal for administrative winding up, i.e. the liquidation decided by the owners themselves (the State represented by SPF and then by APMSP).

Obviously, the administrative winding up is the only solution for the time being, the only way of speeding up restructuring or even of initiating it since more often than not both the bad payers and the creditors are State organizations. However, with increase of the privatization degree in industry, the creditors have to assume their essential role in restructuring.

At present, market economy cannot close down factories in Romania. There are still ruins from the command economy and typical situations that cannot be solved based on the criteria of market economy only. On the other hand, they might be if unemployment quotas higher than 20–30% would be accepted.

Therefore, between the two extremes – to do nothing or the hypothetical one involving 20–30% unemployment quotas – a realistic restructuring should be adopted, based on the market signals but leaving also space for direct government intervention. The present results emphasize such a conclusion.

CHAPTER 23

The only results: in mining

The only concrete results where got in restructuring mining: they were spectacular on a short term and disastrous on a long term.

Incredible situations appeared: miners barricaded themselves in mines asking to be discharged; mangers and trade-union leaders asking together the government to stop redundancy that would leave them without employees.

Ciorbea government embarked upon a terrible adventure: to restructure mining. The consequences were almost unimaginable.

Everything started from the ordinance according to which the miners were to receive at once the whole amount of money they were entitled to following redundancy. A genial solution for a short-term approach. What seemed to last years was solved in no time.

An impressive sociological phenomenon appeared: tens of thousands Moldavians – who had come during communism to the mining areas – took their money, sold their flats for a washing machine or refrigerator, and returned to their native villages. Many of them wanted to embark on farming; others hoped to live on the interests of the money they had deposited that sometimes represented the equivalent of a monthly wage. Too few thought to set up their own business.

The funds for paying all that money came partly from unemployment benefit funds, partly from the State budget that was allowed to collect 70% of the amounts got from privatization. Both risky and wrong, because the privatization money does not belong to consumption but to long-term investments. It is hard to say if now it was or was not worth changing its destination: the mining problem was solved in

Romania in no time, whereas in other countries it took long years.

However, the big problem was the fate of those who, having not a better alternative, made redundant themselves. Eventually money ended and in some areas in Moldova unemployment rate was higher than anywhere else in Romania.

Programs of workforce re-conversion should have been started at once in those areas and fiscal and customs facilities should have been initiated for encouraging investments. Unfortunately, Ciorbea government started such an ample action both logistically unprepared and without enough money.

Concretely, what seemed extremely difficult, even impossible, soon became accomplished fact.

Coal and non-ferrous mining is non-profitable in Romania. The coal is both qualitatively poorer and more expensive than the imported one; at the same time, it has no market (it exceeds the amount used for producing electricity, the only field in which it can be used). Another aggravating factor was emphasized by the 1997 redundancy: extremely low labor productivity.

The only solution in these conditions was to close down the most non-profitable mines both to significantly reduce losses and to downsize coal production. Redundancy was thus a normal follow up.

Since no other solution existed, the only thing subject to negotiations was the social problem. Realistically, since those areas were mono-industrial, the State should have invested directly there. Unfortunately, the government had not the necessary money and the Romanian State should have made external credits.

Instead, the redundant miners received compensations. Although such rewards were specially invented for miners, they were generalized and became the very logo of restructuring by demolition, without reconstruction.

Generally, such compensations should have been avoided since they represent rather a bribe than a real instrument of action and are practically wasted money that created expensive and aggressive unemployed people who hardly agreed to take other jobs.

CHAPTER 24

Failure in the oil refineries sector

Restructuring oil refineries should have been one of the priorities of the Romanian economy. Romania has an oil refining capacity for 32 million tons crude oil although the domestic requirements are 12–13 million tons (14–16 million according to other opinions). Romania's domestic production is about 6 million tons. Now, is it profitable for Romania to use the exceeding refining capacity for processing imported crude oil and for exporting oil products (admitting that business partners can be found)? Otherwise, the exceeding refining capacities should be reduced.

Refining means crude oil separation into several fractions: light (gaseous: butane and propane, liquids: high-octane gasoline), medium (kerosene, paraffin), and heavy (oils and fuel). The resulting products do not correspond exactly to the demand structure (heavier structures are used in thermo-power stations, gasoline for internal combustion engines, etc.). That is why, another more expensive and complex distillation is necessary: catalytic cracking. The products thus obtained are industrial, not power-related.

Therefore, refining is just a technological stage (an essential one) in processing oil to be used for providing energy or in industry. Oil processing means also use of the resulting products in petrochemical industry, chemistry, and plastics industry, medicine industry – branches not well developed in Romania. Thus, the refining capacity of a country is appreciated starting from the domestic demand; the fractions that cannot be covered by that capacity are imported.

No country builds up more refining capacities than its domestic requirements, no matter if the crude oil is imported or not. It is not profitable. Refining produces willy-nilly more than 80 products: some of them can be sold abroad, some others, not. Transportation is difficult and expensive. Oil producing and exporting countries export crude oil, not oil products because their refining capacities tally with their consumptions and not with their productions.

No country develops its refining capacities to export refined oil products. Nobody has ever done it, except Ceausescu who wrongly thought that it was worthy.

Practically, Romania has to give up its exceeding refining capacity. However, it tried to privatize it. Privatization might be a solution if the main refineries "externalize" crude oil supply and oil derivatives sale, and only processing points remain for processing imported oil for foreign markets. Unfortunately, there are just two such refineries: Petrotel and Petromidia. All the problems generated by the huge difference between the refining capacity and the market requirements have remained with no solution. The future is still vague: Romania might process the Caucasian oil in its presumptive way to Western Europe, but this is still a hypothesis.

For the time being, Romania imports as much crude oil as it can and the largest part of refineries, State or private, work under capacity, namely at a loss.

CHAPTER 25

In utilities: change of labels

However, the most important failure was that in utilities, where nothing but names or labels were generally changed. The only exceptions, Romtelecom and the Bucharest water network, are rather privatization counterarguments than arguments.

The initial and major impediment in restructuring this sector was its "monopoly" status (autonomous (State) companies): it was placed under government supervision and considered "unalienable" property.

Protected by their status, the autonomous companies consolidated their political-managerial-trade-unionist structure, subject to cliental politics, and became the most effective instruments of spending public funds. Consequently, they were the most resistant nucleus against any change.

The best example is the national electricity company – RENEL – that became the most important national company in Romania, the exclusive supplier of electricity. Although it was not a monopoly in thermal energy supply, it had exclusivity for large urban areas. At the same time, it was a monopoly of coal and the most important customer of the natural gas exploited or imported by Romania.

The general perception was that RENEL used its monopolist position to impose high prices for both electricity and heat, and contractual conditions that stipulated obligations for its customers only. More than that, despite the high prices imposed, RENEL excessively spent public funds and never paid back either to the State budget or to the social insurance budget. Consequently, RENEL became the greatest debtor company. Finally, RENEL was overstaffed and paid very good wages to its people: a cleaning person had a better wage than a minister.

Who could have been then interested in RENEL restructuring? Quite the opposite. A genuine managerial-trade-unionist plot was organized to keep the whole mechanism as such and to ensure RENEL a relative prosperity in contradiction with the deep poverty around. The managers were interested in keeping their peace and security and in avoiding all the concerns of the managers in other companies that had to face competition.

On the other hand, the trade-union leaders risked to face the dilemma "higher wages or more staff" and to lose their allies – the employers – together with which they blackmailed the government. As they could not expose their true reasons against change, both managers and trade unions invoked increase in costs, consumers' disadvantages, lower exploitation security, etc.

25.1. Market behavior or a government instrument?

Breaking such a mechanism was just one side of RENEL restructuring; on the other side, the government (whatever its color) should have changed its position towards RENEL. The governments permanently used RENEL as a social and economic instrument in the field of employing workforce, fuels, prices administration, control of currency funds, etc. The State controlled and approved all the decisions concerning budget, investments, and allocations to RENEL. In fact, RENEL was a kind of bank for industry and for other State-owned companies. What else could be called the system of "cross subventions" according to which the economic organizations had to pay RENEL higher prices so that RENEL might sell cheaper to the population? If the government wanted social security, it should have used the budget, not RENEL! On the other hand, the interdiction imposed when RENEL wanted to stop supplying the economic organizations that had not paid for their heat and electricity invoices was just another tool for implementing government politics. Thus, RENEL became one of the most profitable banks in Romania from where its customers could borrow, without giving the money back. Another bank, similarly profitable was only the State budget!

Concretely, what exactly meant the change of RENEL into CONEL, and of the latter into five distinct companies, according to the principle "production – transportation – distribution": Termoelectrica, Hidroelectrica, and Nuclearoelectrica (each a monopoly in electricity production from thermal, hydro-, and nuclear sources, respectively), Transcom (transportation), and Electrica (the monopoly in distribution). The only change was a principle one and with a possible long-term impact: the company property was no longer public and unalienable; it might have become – partially or totally – privatized.

The case of the electricity company is not singular. The same thing happened with the company for producing and distributing methane gas where differences still exist between the prices paid by the economic organizations and the price paid by the population, and where the interdiction to stop delivery to bad payers is still in force.

Obviously, genuine restructuring should suppose independence of these companies (whatever their names) and market behavior. In such a case, the State should solve the problem of those that do not pay their electricity and gas invoices – companies or private persons – but it cannot because there is no money. Therefore, utilities restructuring is a matter of political will and of money alike.

Something has to change in the field of utilities and rather quickly. To replace a State company with a private one would solve nothing. It would use the same strategy of transferring its internal or external problems to the delivery price, instead of trying to reduce operation costs or to become competitive. In a completely anti-economic approach, when consumption drops because of high prices, the respective monopolies respond by increasing prices, instead of reducing them. To the end of the previous decade, the consumption practically collapsed whereas prices reached astronomical figures.

25.2. "De-monopolization" is a must!

De-monopolization is the only way out. The solution generally suggested is "dismantling" of the present national companies that now integrate production, transportation, and distribution of the main public utilities. Generally, privatization would aim at the production and distribution segments; transportation could remain public property.

The opponents of giving up State companies attack this "segmentation" and their arguments are not few, from endangering exploitation security to losing control of prices (out of social reasons). However, the situation in the latest years is the best counterargument: lower demand, higher prices, and poorer quality. The opponents of "segmentation" could invoke something else: nowadays, a merging fever has seized the business world. Globalization "calls" for the giant companies to unify their forces and face both competition and the huge costs of adapting to new technologies.

Faced with these tendencies, "segmentation" seems rather obsolete. Unfortunately, the change of inefficient giants into efficient ones cannot be made just like that. The world mergers take place among prosperous companies that aim at a better competitiveness, and involve downsizing and redundancies for a better profitability. In Romania, "dismantling" is sometimes the only solution for breaking inefficient, State monopolies.

Obviously, neither "dismantling" nor privatizations are goals in themselves. At present, the utilities have objectively and unavoidably become open sectors, and "segmentation" and privatization are the ways that make them open to competition. Nobody can say that beneficial result will appear by applying the "segmentation-privatization" binomial. However, the disastrous effects recorded up to now are enough reasons to believe that such a move is worth trying.

CHAPTER 26

The sketch of "restructuring without money"

No industrial restructuring has been made in Romania. The first Iliescu administrations did not even want to. They preserved the whole industry as such and finally compromised it.

Neither did RDC-DP coalition restructure industry. Practically, they made a kind of de-industrialization. It is very well to close down non-profitable companies, to downsize the non-functional sector, and to give up energy consuming industries, but we have to put something else instead.

For 12 long years, all the governments avoided to demolish what had to be finally demolished with the only result that the social and economic costs kept increasing.

The involvement of the World Bank in the restructuring process in Romania had a positive aspect through their permanent pressure on the Romanian authorities to deal with the problem directly. However, the results, or better the lack of results, should be considered.

The credits granted by the World Bank for specific projects, of the so-called "structural adjustment" (FESAL, then PSAL), concentrated on restructuring non-profitable organizations, were not a success whatsoever. Long years of experience demonstrated that such general and not punctual programs were doomed.

Their approach was too simplistic: privatization or, if no buyer appears, liquidation! As nobody ever thought of putting something instead, liquidation was suspected, debts increased and privatization chances became almost zero.

The structural adjustment programs agreed with the World Bank had two components: massive and imperative "purging" and presumptive construction.

The purging component included: demolition in the non-functional sector, liquidation of the loss-generating organizations, and social security; also, the so-called banks restructuring, in fact transferring the non-performing credits (credit losses) from the State banks to public funds. Of course, everything costs: demolition, social security, and mainly bank restructuring. All in all, about several billions dollars, not just several hundreds dollars, the financial assistance offered by the World Bank.

The latter component, construction, included: programs for workforce reconversion; the creation of a stimulating business environment; and construction by privatization. As privatization would be the only part able to support construction and the only one supposed to bring some money, the whole construction is presumptive. Privatization is not certitude, and certainly is will not be a rapid process.

In ex-East Germany, the success in economic restructuring was supported by about DM 1 000 billion external resources, and in Hungary by more than $30 billion. Thus, to restructure the Romanian economy with several hundreds of millions dollars (as stipulated in the programs agreed with the World Bank) would be either poor joke or just miracle. Unfortunately, nobody works miracles and restructuring can be made with money only.

Therefore, we should admit the failure of the restructuring programs. Together with the World Bank, some other kind of programs should be adopted for solving punctually the cases of the problem-organizations, taking into account the sector they belong to and their location. The new program could use the World Bank resources to close down loss-generating factories and to set up viable alternatives.

CHAPTER 27

A "nonstructural" unemployment

In 2000, about 1 200 000 persons were unemployed in Romania, representing about 12% of the workforce total – the highest percent recorded after 1989. In 2001, there were 8%. Is it much; is it not? The short answer is: it is not, but it is disastrous.

A restructuring country must have unemployment. A high unemployment rate is both unavoidable and healthy for a short time. Considering the ample structural changes required by the Romanian economy, 10–12% is a small figure that shows that the changes are not as ample as they should be. The even smaller figures, 6–8%, recorded for several years indicated that the structural economic reforms were delayed for too long. Likewise, the promises made by Nastase government to reduce unemployment reveal that they do not have in view significant restructuring.

About 20–25% unemployment quotas would project a structural change, closer to the requirements of the Romanian economy.

However, the Romanian unemployment is disastrous because it is not the result of economic restructuring but of economic demolition. Therefore, it is not a structural unemployment, an objective, and temporary one, generated by changing sectors, activities, and professions. Structural unemployment is necessary in restructuring countries – in fact restructuring is a permanent process – because declining sectors and activities produce unemployed, who are then absorbed by the developing sectors and activities.

In Romania, the declining sectors and activities are maintained by political and electoral interests, and no new sectors and activities are created. The unemployment resulted from demolition without reconstruction is a hard to absorb one.

The present state of things has another serious consequence. Without significant investments, nobody can configure either the amplitude of the workforce demand in the future or the professional structure of that demand. Therefore, neither workforce reconversion programs nor school can make the most realistic offers for the future.

CHAPTER 28

Anti-economy in the power-sector

The situation in the power sector best characterizes the present Romanian economy. The national power sector is in crises: not because it cannot meet the demand, but because there is no demand. Practically, because of the frequent and huge price hikes, neither population nor industry can pay. A remarkable achievement indeed! During 1997–2000, the electricity price increased 16 times, whereas the prices increased generally only 7.7 times, and the *leu* devalued 7 times. The situation continued after 2000 as well: energy prices (electricity, thermal, and natural gas) exceeded 56% compared with 30% for other prices in 2001.

Apparently, the situation had been dramatic before 1989 as well. However, the reasons were quite different then. Ceausescu had created an extremely large energy-consuming industry for a country with poor resources. The imported ones were very expensive. The non-functional industry could not export enough to get the hard currency necessary for importing the power resources. Just another vicious circle!

Following 1989, no strategy was conceived to improve that situation: neither energy-consuming industry nor the energy production sector was improved.

Since nothing was done for restructuring industry and production, the power system simply drifted along with the trends in economy that almost "swallowed" it up.

For a short time, decrease in industrial production was felt as a relief. However, very soon, the few exports collapsed and the poor currency resources for power imports ceased to exist.

To overcome difficulties, Vacaroiu government conceived a system by which the State covered yearly the price difference of the power sold at a loss. For the power imports necessary for winter, money was borrowed from Bancorex and the debt was paid in 1999, when the bank broke and the bankruptcy was transferred to the public debts. Good deal indeed! Industry consumed and population paid.

When the RDC-DP coalition took over power, the World Bank and IMF specifically asked that power should not be delivered at a loss. Simultaneously, a mechanism was conceived for automatically indexing the energy price in agreement with currency devaluation. Good measures, but as neither consuming industry nor energy production were restructured, everything turned into disaster.

However, nobody dared introduce the principle "the consumer pays" and sell the energy at its real price.

Thus, a "cross subvention" system was adopted and the economic organizations had to pay more for a so-called protection of the population. A false protection anyhow since population had to pay finally more for other products and services delivered by the former. The system was dangerous and compromised real long-term solutions.

The energy consumption decreased drastically and in 1997–2000 the monopolist electricity company used the indexation mechanism to fabulously increase the prices, exceeding the *leu* devaluation they should have followed.
In the cold months, the electricity and heat invoices were higher than the average incomes of the greatest part of the Romanians – a pure economic anomaly. The effect was that the heat and electricity suppliers, using their monopolist positions, increased prices and defied reality, and the population became poorer and poorer.

An economic program in which the power invoices for population are higher than the average incomes per family is doomed to fail. Even if such a program completely ignores social objectives and makes a fetish of certain economic fixities it finally blocks off its own way: population cannot pay off their invoices and economy stalls.

Why are the invoices so expensive in comparison with incomes? On the one hand, because of lack of efficiency in production and distribution of the supplying companies, because of their monopolist positions that allow them to have huge incomes, and because of the bad-paying industrial consumers. On the other hand, because of the enormous losses in the distribution networks (supported by consumers, of course). That is why the central administration of distributing heat is against de-branching: those having heat meters pay exactly what they consume while those paying for losses are fewer.

As the power suppliers can so easily increase delivery prices, they are not interested in reducing costs by giving up inefficient production units, now completely useless following consumption collapse with more than 30% after 1989. Thus, the way was open to anti-economy. Prices increase whereas demand decreases. Arrears keep accumulating because economy and population can no longer pay the invoices. The electricity company does no longer pay its suppliers and uses the little money it cashes to increase wages.

After long years of economic and social policy made through the national electricity company, the government does not dare ask the company restructuring.

The Romanians cannot get rid soon of the huge electric invoices. A genuine solution can only be found on a long term or a very long term only. This would mean, first, a sound economic growth, the only one able to allow higher wages and pensions, and, second, "de-monopolization" of power production and distribution.

CHAPTER 29

Privatization without buyers or an absurd theatre

Doubtlessly, the privatization in Romania is a failure. The privatization quota is minimal and the rhythm is very slow. However, the most serious aspect is that the wages in the privatized companies are no higher than the State ones. Therefore, nobody can come with a successful privatization story and say: "that's the best example."

To the end of 2000, i.e. in eight years since it had been set up, SPF (then APMSP) – a special privatization organization – had privatized only 44% of its assets. As SPF took over only 45% of the whole State companies, Romania had privatized only 19% of its State productive organizations by the end of 2000. Therefore, there is no wonder that Romanian economy is disastrous.

29.1. Legal and institutional confusions

The failure has multiple causes. First, the legal and administrative status of the industrial property is rather vague. The legal framework was not conceived to make privatization easier but to delay it and it soon became a genuine obstacle due to its confusing nature.

The source of all confusions was the law governing trading companies, promoted by Petre Roman government in 1990. The law granted autonomy to the State organizations re-called "trading companies" that could be privatized in principle, unlike the autonomous (State) companies that remained public property and could not be privatized. In fact, nobody was responsible for the "independent" trading companies. Practically, no one represented the owner-State.

The privatization law, adopted in 1991, opened a wider way to disaster: 70% of the capital to be privatized was given to SPF (State Property Fund) and the remaining 30% was to be distributed freely to adult population. SPF had to privatize the capital it owned, therefore to do something that menaced its very existence. Logically, the SPF staff did their best to stop their organization perform the very task it had been set up for.

Likewise, SPF was not the legal representative of the owner-State, but a shareholder only, and acted as the State representative only when such a position was convenient (when it privatized). It pretended to be just a shareholder in the current management of its own industrial capital and declined any responsibility whatsoever in the economic results; when no prospect existed in stopping losses and overdue payments, it simply liquidated the company. Such a decision would be normal in the case of any owner broken and assaulted by debtors. According to law, SPF was not forced to take over losses or to respond for the overdue payments. So, why should it have privatized? The only one made responsible was the government – although it did not represent the owner-State – and finally the population had to pay for the losses.

The confusion in assuming responsibilities and taking decisions was even greater when the mass privatization program was applied: following subscriptions, SPF maintained only the relative majority of the capital in numerous organizations and lost the absolute one.

When nobody knows exactly who the owner is and what is the exact situation of the property, the buyers hesitate. More than that so when the properties have so many problems and there is nobody to discuss them with.

The problems are huge and serious: who is responsible for the debts accumulated by those companies?; has anybody the right to exempt part of the debts or to reschedule them? No possible buyer could discuss such problems with SPF. The case of the failed privatization of Resita Steel Combine Works is highly significant. SPF negotiated with the buyer, the American company "Noble Ventures," facilities (debt exemptions and rescheduling) concerning the "historical debts" of the organizations. Finally, the government agreed with all these facilities. When the administration changed, the new government did not agree with the old terms. Under the new conditions, the American company did not pay wages, the workers blocked off the public roads, and finally the government sued "Noble Ventures" and asked for the annulment of the privatization contract.

In fact, SPF was a happy shareholder, completely unaffected by the losses of its companies. No creditor – supplier, bank, or State budget – could make SPF legally responsible because those companies did not pay their debts. When a debt-related problem appeared, SPF directed it to the government that had no connection with the owner-State, but could only reschedule or waive part of the budget debts of a company that might have found a buyer. Obviously, if anyone had tried to detangle the confused legal and administrative rigmarole, several long years would have been necessary. However, such a thing would have been possible even taking into account the excessive Romanian paperwork and bureaucracy.

29.2. Mishmash of FIS's

What happened with the remaining 30% of the capital to be taken by the adult Romanians? Since the shares could not be distributed individually, five institutions called Private Property Funds (PPF) were invented to take care of the above percent until the shares had been distributed. If the process had lasted, let us say, six months, there would have been no problem. However, since the law deliberately stipulated no time limit, the staff working there (employed following political criteria) had every interest to delay it as much as possible. As the process lasted five years, they had plenty of time to buy expensive cars and to build elegant office buildings with the population's money. In exchange, the adult population received no dividends, although they were shareholders.

When the mass privatization process finally ended, FPP's changed into FIS – financial investments societies – that pretended to be private. Why and how private? They were set up as a State "gift," gave nothing to the population, and the "capitalists" working there took care of their interest only. In addition, the action was legal!

Finally, only 21% of 30% was distributed to population; the rest is at FIS's disposal (possession!).

FIS's simply defied the Romanian people and are the greatest shame of the Romanian capitalism. State-gifted capitalism is not capitalism but a kind of mishmash. There are so many private structures oppressed by unfriendly laws and ruining taxes. FIS's, on the other hand, are protected by all kind of regulations that turned them into genuine fortresses nobody can touch.

Their main weapons are the shares they have in banks, a part of the gift they received years before. During five years of managing the population's property without giving anything in exchange, they actually used the money they won to consolidate their portfolios in bank. More than that, FIS's did not accept any kind of compensating shares exchanges with SPF, as stipulated by the initial law of banks privatization. Later on, when unwise management broke so many banks, FIS's, as stakeholders, did not want to accept the losses in the banks where they had shares in. In fact, what did FIS's want when they tried to stop the privatization of the Agricola Bank by suing it? Just to be exempted of the Bank's losses. They asked that only the institutions representing the Romanian State should take over the losses and wanted in exchange other more profitable shares in the banking or in the insurance sector.

29.3. Privatization of profits and nationalization of losses

Privatization of profits and nationalization of losses were both made in the mentioned time interval. Political-managerial-trade-union structures seized the State organizations, "slices" of exports and imports were given within a cliental system, and private and legal persons simply robbed State banks by not paying their debts. Practically, small private groups confiscated all profits. However, all the losses in economy resulted both from inefficient companies or bad management and from thefts were "nationalized" and the population had to pay for them. In 1996, at the end of his mandate, Prime Minister Vacaroiu deployed the fact that whereas 90% of the exported products came from the State sector, more than 50% of the profits were taken in "transit" by private companies that, obviously, took over the goods, probably in books only.

Unfortunately, the RDC-DP coalition did not find the best way for privatization. They wanted to demonstrate that success can be reached rapidly and started privatizing profitable, easy to sell organizations, instead of looking for solutions and buyers for problematic organizations. Therefore, they made a kind of privatization for privatization's sake, with small returns for relatively profitable companies, whereas the unprofitable ones remained in the SPF property and kept on accumulating debts.

The Romtelecom privatization might be the emblematic example – a huge failure. First, because the monopoly of the Romanian State in this field was conceded to another State: OTE, the buyer is the property of Greece. Second, the buyer was granted the right to keep monopoly for another five years. Third, the price – $ 675 million – was too small, about half the real one and aroused the suspicion that important commissions entered unofficially the pockets of the Romanian officials who approved such a transaction. Romtelecom was by far the most profitable Romanian organization and the Romanian State gave it away without recovering at least the money invested to update the networks.

29.4. The cost of the delaying tactics

Romtelecom is the typical example of such a tactics for which the vendor-State in this case had to pay dearly: they got a too small price. Obviously, if Romtelecom had been privatized in 1994–1995, when the Romanian telephonic networks were down and when the international investors were interested in the Central and East-European area the potential profit would have been huge. In 1998, when the investment climate had become depressive, when the economic prospects of the whole area were much doubted, and when Romania was at the top of the distrust list, following permanent deterioration of its economy, the situation was completely changed. The country-risk demotions prohibitively increased prices or even forbade access to international capital markets and diminished the prices the State could get from privatizations.

When Romtelecom was privatized, mobile phone companies had already entered Romania and extended rapidly, thus reducing the business opportunity envisaged by Romtelecom privatization.

It is obvious that Romania lacked a general privatization strategy, agreed upon by all political forces. The same happened with the money got from privatizations.

PSDR administration in 1992–1996 considered that the money should be used exclusively for investments and for restructuring: projects or restructuring programs. They also agreed with the scheme of the highest returns (60%) to the buyer for supporting after-privatization restructuring.

The RDC-DP administration did not agree with the above scheme; they said that it would spread even more confusion in deciding the privatizing prices and it would be useless to include it in the contracts with foreign partners. Likewise, they considered that the financings hidden under the noble goal of supporting restructuring simply meant to waste money in bankrupt companies. Therefore, RDC-DP coalition changed the privatization returns and directed the money to the State budget. An uninspired solution, since the money was used for consumption and not for productive investments.

However, following PSDR delaying tactics and the rush of the RDC-DP administration, Romania reached a deadlock: it had more debts than assets and it was rather difficult to find buyers for the privatizing organizations.

In 2000, the new PSDR administration changed again the privatization regulations, besides the new name given to SPF that became the Authority for Privatization and Management of State Participations (APMSP). They added the clause of maintaining the area of activity for at least five years and at least 70% of the turnover before privatization. Another clause was to underwrite shares of the bought portfolio for the investments assumed after privatization. Penalties of up to 30% were stipulated for each term default and if the shares were too few, the buyers were forbidden to sell or to mortgage the assets they had bought. They wanted a kind of gradual privatization: the buyers had no full rights until they had honored all their commitments. Likewise, the buyers had to pay all the compensating wages in case of collective redundancy, the national insurances, and jobseeker's allowances.

They intended to set up a National Restructuring Fond for restructuring organizations to be privatized. However, the international financial organizations did not agree and the money got from privatizations was to be used concretely for redeeming the public debts.

Although the Nastase government projects were OK, the problem was quite different: the privatization in Romania was in acute crisis.

29.5. Price limits are very low

The privatization in Romania was badly conceived by Petre Roman government, was delayed during the first PSDR administration, and speeded up by the RDC–DP coalition. Therefore, it was doomed and has no chance of redressing. It has to face insoluble problems and there is no hope of success: prices will be lower and lower and the after-privatizations conditions will be worse. The Romanian organizations are ten years older now and there is no money for updating them. Many of them have no longer markets. Therefore, their equipments are worthless stuff and not a component of the privatization price. Their debts are a burden and the prospective buyers do not want to commit themselves. Consequently, prices can be only small irrespective of negotiations.

Under such conditions, the measures taken by Nastase government, although apparently correct and justified, might have no contribution to speeding up privatization. But for the necessary penalties against the investors who breach their contracts, the new regulations simply add further obstacles: the investors who care about their money will never accept to buy a company and not to be allowed to change its activity for five years or to be forced to keep redundant staff when this very activity or the very redundant staff explains the disastrous situation of that company. No investor will accept to become a gradual owner!

The absence of buyers and not bad or good regulations represent the privatization crisis in Romania. The domestic private capital cannot update the big State companies and the foreign private capitals cannot be interested to face so many problems. They want profit only.

SIDEX privatization represented the crucial test for the fate of privatization in Romania. The privatization of the Galati Steel Combine Works was a major stake: the change of the disastrous game rules in the Romanian economy. Once started, the change could no longer be stopped. SIDEX was the very center of that game, harmful for the Romanian State and for the Romanians alike; it was the keystone for the great money transfers to falsely social purposes, the instrument of the pork-barrel politics, the knot of the huge diversion called "financial blockage", and the very nucleus of the hybrid economy (neither command nor market) that hindered Romanian economy to be a market economy.

SIDEX became the classical example of the crooked market economy in Romania. A genuine privatization of SIDEX would have been a serious blow on that grotesque system.

Privatization should have been made almost irrespective of the price. Likewise, issues transcending Romania had to be considered. For all the countries, steel is a "strategic" activity, controlled by the domestic capitals. Consequently, the world steel market is rather fragmented. On the other hand, the world markets of iron ore and those of machine building (mainly cars) are completely monopolized – they are dominated by five or six "players" – and the tendency exists to rapidly consolidate the steel market. There is no other choice than to be in or out the world steel market. That was the stake of SIDEX being bought by one of those concerns. There was only one prospective buyer – the Indian-British concern LNM-ISPAT. A great opportunity indeed.

The only problem was if Nastase government had the courage to cut the Gordian knot. Fortunately, Nastase government passed the test.

CHAPTER 30

Agriculture – neither fish nor flesh

"Neither fish nor flesh" best characterizes the reform in agriculture where the half measures were completely unfit. Agriculture was the field in which the failure of the communist collectivization was the most dramatic one, probably because it broke the most intimate connection – material and spiritual alike – with private property.

30.1. Hesitating and partial reconstitution of private property

A rapid reconstitution of private property was essential in agriculture. The associations could have been more efficient, but the owners were strictly fictitious and their motivation was entirely compromised. Other ex-communist countries (Czech Republic or Hungary) did not face such acute problems because the motivation for working in agricultural cooperatives had not been destroyed.

Although imperious and extremely important, the reconstitution of the private property in agriculture was hesitating from the very beginning: it started in a rush, but it was an extremely harmful half measure.

The 1991 law of land property was a simple "re-individualization" of the private land the ex-owners had been forced to work collectively. The ex-properties were given back only within a 10-ha limit.

The State property (agricultural State enterprises having almost 30% of the whole land, obviously the best one) was not privatized and the ex-owners could only become shareholders to a certain extent. The argument for keeping that property was that the respective land would ensure continuity and provide the food for townies. However, the real reason was that the fresh post-December officials did not want to give up State property and they refused the very principle of retrocession.

Without retrocession, agriculture could not start working on a market economy basis: no land market could be created and it was impossible to stop the counterproductive fragmentation of the land into small plots initiated by the 1991 law.

The title deeds were not given back because of the delays in enforcing land law, and also because of the law intricacies that generated more than 600 000 litigations.

Likewise, at the beginning, the law said nothing about the agricultural inputs privatization. Therefore, agricultural machinery remained in the State property and was destroyed or stolen: just another obstacle against the development of agriculture.

During its first administration, PSDR tried to save the dying State agriculture by massive and expensive subsidies, with no success whatsoever. The losses in the State agriculture and in animal husbandry were higher than ever and accumulated huge arrears.

Unfortunately, the World Bank financed the subsidizing that became a strong inflation source as well.

30.2. A natural-type economy

In the meantime, a large part of the private agriculture, facing lack of money and of agricultural machinery, became a natural-type economy. Small production became the most important segment in the private agriculture. This type of farming does not use industrial products and services because of their high prices, has relatively few connections with the market, prefers barter instead of money, and has no connection whatsoever with the banks. Generally, this kind of production is not for the market or has no connection with market. Anyhow, the unorganized and unaudited peasant market took over a large part of the town customers within the audited and taxed system. The too great weight of food expenses – because of the generally low incomes – within the general marketing of the Romanians thus explains why the whole trading system of the audited economy collapsed, mainly in the sales of consumer goods.

Another serious consequence of the prohibiting prices of industrial products and services used in agriculture is the almost exclusive field cultures of corn and wheat that grow easily and are essential for the farmers' own consumption. Unfortunately, the corn-wheat cycle with no fertilizers severely compromised numerous plots in several of the best agricultural areas of Romania.

30.3. The failure of the National Peasant Party

The RDC–PD coalition (1996–2000) had overwhelming tasks in agriculture: to finalize land retrocession; to stop subsidizing agriculture with inflation money; to privatize State agriculture; to privatize cereals gathering and storage; to privatize agricultural machinery; and to liberalize prices and foreign trade with agricultural produces.

Their administration had good and bad points and was highly controversial. In both directions – the good and the bad one – they were influenced by the ASAL agreement concluded with the World Bank that imposed it to Ciorbea government.

The most important failure was in land retrocession. Retrocession had been the electoral slogan of the coalition majority but they did not succeed in giving back the land they had promised.

The regrettable obstructions of DP, the similarly regrettable ambiguities of NLP, and the rigidity of NPP in applying a certain solution explain their failure. According to the protocol signed by the coalition forces in 1997, what was in the State property in 1945, when the agrarian reform law was passed, remained to the State (about 200 000 ha). To that, the Crown estate and what was later gained following land reclaims added. The difference owned by the ex-State agricultural units (more than 1.6 million ha) could be and had to be given back. The retrocession limit was 50 ha for the ex-owners or their descendants. Therefore, the "danger" of reconstituting the ex-landowners' properties was a mere political and electoral bogey. There was enough land for everybody and if there was not, the solution was simple: they had to retrocede the existing land. Practically, the retrocession was blocked by group or personal interests. Unfortunately, the Democratic Party needed long years to stop such people as Trita Fanita, a member of the party, who obstructed the law helped by the very ambiguities within the party. Trita Fanita, together with other Romanian grain wholesalers, needed the State agricultural units to trade, with small expenses and little concern, corn and wheat. Why should have he collected grain from farmers, who were spread over a larger territory, when it was so simple to deal directly with the State units?

30.4. Was State agriculture good?

In his attempt to stop the adoption of the retrocession law, Trita Fanita supported the idea that the State should keep its property or *"that wealth of the Romanians would otherwise go to hell."* Was agricultural State property a good thing?

The State property and the generalized nationalization of agriculture seem to have been the most serious failure of communism. Let us remember the food shortage and the long lines of people waiting to buy food in Romania. What was good in that? Comparison with the present shows what can do private property in agriculture, incompletely reinstated as it is. Subsidizations of thousands of billions *lei* were wasted on the State lands during the first PSDR administration with no success whatsoever: production was low and the population had to pay for the money borrowed from the Agricola Bank to support the State agriculture but filled other pockets.

The RDC–DP administration is responsible for the failure in privatizing ex-ASU's (Agricultural State Units). Besides the clans of wholesalers, new clans of village barons appeared. While the former fight for defending State property, the latter have a more capitalistic vision: they fight for ASU's privatization and want to foist their conditions on the market.

The RDC–DP coalition adopted the law that permitted land sale and purchase, and opened the way to a land market. It is however interesting that all the political forces agreed that the private properties should not exceed 200 ha although they all had agreed that the ex-landowners' properties should be retroceded within a 50-ha limit. Therefore, an ex-landowner's property should be of 50 ha the most, whereas the property of a nouveau riche can have 200 ha!

30.5. Is food security a forgotten goal?

Highly controversial are the other stipulations in the ASAL agreement as well: reorganization by limiting the system of security reserves and privatization or liquidation of the State units for growing pigs and chickens.

The ASAL program established a wheat security reserve of only 350 000 tons, about 10% of Romania's yearly consumption despite the "normal" limit of 20 % the least. The explanation was that such stocks were too expensive. For "limit-situations" and emergencies, an account was opened with $ 60-million credit from the World Bank. Concretely, there existed a good stock, but it was limited and loans for emergencies were made – everything in good order with the agreement of the World Bank and of Ciorbea government.

More than that, exactly when the security stocks were given up, they adopted the decision for liberalizing exports. Therefore, a good measure in principle could have become a danger to food security.

ASAL agreement seems to have forgotten the food security – a fundamental aspect observed in all the other countries. Simultaneously, for the sudden and massive decrease of the customs duties the explanation was given that the imports pressure could stimulate domestic production and lower costs.

Likewise, massive and sudden diminution of the customs duties for food products is undoubtedly crucial in promoting competition and performance in agriculture, and in preparing it for the possible integration into the European Union. However, such a dramatic diminution is made when the domestic production is sound; it is not the case of the Romanian agriculture where land is still tilled with oxen and horses.

The pig and chicken farms suffered the greatest losses. Many of them became completely uninteresting for the investors and had to be liquidated.

30.6. About food imports

The effects of liberalization are hard to appreciate. Generally, the official statistics offer one fragment of reality only: the people in town and cities that buy audited food only, no matter if it is imported or not. Therefore, such statistics showing the contribution of food imports to the population's consumption are not relevant since in villages – with about 45% of the whole population – self-consumption is predominant and an important part of the townies buy from the unaudited market.

The statistics show that the increase of the food imports is nothing to worry about: about 30% between 1997 and 2000, following the very low level of imports in 1997. Compared to 1995, there was no increase in 2000.

The main shock of liberalizations appeared in 1991–1995; the foreign trade stopped being a monopoly and food imports increased very much with a peak in 1995.

Liberalization of foreign trade following 1990 caused massive and sudden increase of food imports, that had been forbidden in Romania (for example, exotic fruits), and of other more competitive aliments.

The Romanian farming is highly inefficient because of the land division into small plots and because of the high prices of the fertilizers and agricultural machinery. Therefore, few Romanian produces can face the competitive imported ones, mainly owing to the extremely low cost of the workforce in Romania.

However, the lack of competitiveness of the Romanian produces is mainly manifested in the collapse of food exports. In 2000, those exports represented less than 30% of the 1995 level and much less than before 1989. A possible explanation could be that Romania used to sell those produces at a loss but it is rather difficult to do the same thing now under the new economic conditions. Prices and foreign trade liberalization,

leu convertibility, price-cost ratios can no longer be ignored, and nobody finances export losses.
Romania is not an exception. Because of their lack of competitiveness, all the underdeveloped countries (we like it or not, Romania is an underdeveloped country) import more produces than they export.

In 1990, when Romania was simply "thrown" in the international competition, the Romanian agriculture faced its own limits and drawbacks. However, Romania changed from a food exporter into a food importer at the end of the administration that kept boasting (and still does) that they supported agriculture, introduced silly customs duties to protect it, and injected huge amounts of money in State agriculture. It was at the end of 1996, following PSDR administration, that food exports simply collapsed and Romania imported 25% more food than it exported. However, PSDR greatest guilt was that they did not concentrate land and agricultural capital on the basis of the market criteria, the only one able to ensure performance and competitiveness in that sector.

Romania will not be able to change the present trends of exports decrease and imports increase until it has made farming competitive. It is however, a long-term process, because industry, the main supplier of farming inputs is also involved. A more immediate solution could be to encourage an industry for processing raw produces for the domestic market at least.

30.7. A tragic inefficiency

The Romanian agriculture has no chance whatsoever if its real problems are not faced.

The most important of them seems to be its lack of efficiency. The farming sector represents about 40% of the workforce but its contribution to GDP is only 12% – a proof of the work low productivity in this sector.

Romania has got almost the best lands in Europe but they give the poorest crops per hectare. Following the 1991 land reform, the property is preponderantly private but the average area of agricultural exploitations is lower than two ha. More than 45% of the owners live in towns and farm for their consumption only in weekends; two thirds of the agricultural exploitations have less than three hectares. Nowhere in the world, can a family live on just 30–40 working days per year. Competitiveness can only be reached by substantial increase of the average area of agricultural exploitation based on higher production yields and better work productivity.

The process was delayed because the landowners did not have to pay taxes and had no obligation towards society. Therefore, the price for such a delay was double. On the one hand, a large part of the Romanian farming returned to a barter-based natural economy and, on the other hand, both external markets and an important sector of the domestic one were lost. The direction of the workforce to agriculture – often considered a solution – is just a temporary palliative and an economic impossibility that could complicate the industry-agriculture relations even more.

These relations tend to become increasingly atypical. The Romanian industry was created and extended at the expense of agriculture. However, the Romanian command industry did not take into account the market signals and now it is not able to stand on its own feet. It is still supported by agriculture although it should have started to help agriculture. However, subsidizing agriculture – through net transfer between economic sectors – is only an illusion in Romania since no sector is able to provide such resources.

30.8. "Wheat crisis" diversion

Each year since 1990, a "wheat crises" has been announced, irrespective of the good or bad crop, of the exports or no exports.

"Wheat crises" has been an ignominious constant of the recent years, loudly announced with the only aim of filling someone's pockets. Farmers themselves have never received the budget money meant to "support agriculture."

Behind the "wheat crises", wholesalers, older or newer village officials, or local barons got substantial contributions sometimes for quite opposite goals: export bonuses and import credits at the same time.

Practically, all the politicians joined them irrespective of their color. Some of them are involved directly, some others do not know exactly what it is all about, but explanations can be easily found. It sounds good to the electorate and 45% of the Romanians live in villages.

Therefore, let us subsidize agriculture! Unfortunately, the politicians are generous with the State money of course because they do not have to offer solutions for the source of money. Neither are the goals to be fulfilled with that money very clear.

30.9. Subsidizing is economically impossible

Almost all politicians say that the industrially developed countries subsidize agriculture. They simply ignore the fact that it is only industrially developed countries that do that because their industries are able to support agriculture. Economically, agriculture cannot be subsidized in Romania because industry has nothing to offer; quite the opposite, it only claims mainly through its unreasonable prices. When the State budget subsidizes agriculture, industry immediately increases the prices of the products and services agriculture needs. From 1990 on, the prices of those services and products have been 1.5 times higher than the prices for produces. In fact, the main issue is not subsidizing agriculture but stopping subjugating it.

Let us admit that funds exist for subsidizing agriculture. Where would they be directed to? To increase wheat production? Can the present production not cover consumption? Even in the worst years, the crop is at least 3 million tons, enough for domestic consumption. If wheat was imported so many times, the reasons were quite different: a better quality of the imported wheat (the Hungarian one, for example), lack of contracting, buying, gathering, and storing systems, and, last but not least, the bribes the importers receive from wheat suppliers.

What happens if crops are better? They will just fill up the barns and remain there. Could we export more? Besides the lack of a proper system for contracting, buying, gathering, and storing, the poor competitiveness has to be considered. What about the world agricultural market? Those who need wheat have no money and those who have money do not need it!

30.10. Supporting performance

Therefore, an increase in crops cannot be the goal if resources for subsidizing agriculture can be found. The only sensible goal could be a more efficient farming. We like it or not, that would suppose bankruptcy of a large part of the present agricultural exploitation and re-direction of the workforce in agriculture to other sectors. The process would be painful but that is another problem.

However, the pain would be less owing to two factors: almost half of the new owners are townies and they will be the first to sell or lease their plots; more than 60% of the people working in agriculture at present are old and their passing away would diminish the tensions generated by a re-orientation of the agricultural workforce. These two factors will soften the initial shock, but after that big economic and social problems will appear.

Which sectors could take over the exodus from agriculture? This might be the most difficult problem since the Romanian economy can no longer provide workplaces.

If the possibility of facing the economic and social problems is not considered there is no other solution left. The Romanian farming products cannot face the foreign, more competitive ones.

The attempt made by Nastase government to introduce "performance-based subsidizing" in agriculture is salutary. Supporting by the State of the agricultural exploitations having more than 110 ha in the plain, 50 ha in the hilly areas, 25 ha in the mountains, and of the animal farms with a numerous livestock is the only viable policy. The opponents have however plenty of counterarguments: The attempt would not aim at a better performance but at supporting the new barons (almost all of them members of Nastase's party), the only ones who own more than 110 ha. Even worse, the harmful ASU's would be again supported with public money. The individual farmers would be forced to make associations – Iliescu's old fixation – and they would be certain victims of the new barons. They will be forced to go to towns that have nothing to offer. There will be victims, but the process will take place willy-nilly. There is no other way. Performance in agriculture and farmers' social security is not possible in Romania at the same time. It is just political hypocrisy and electoral demagogy.

30.11. Prices and underpayment of workforce in agriculture

The idyllic images with farmers coming back to their native villages and working busily their plots of land supported by a fatherly State have no connection with reality whatsoever. The modern and efficient farming does not need many workers, but performing industrial inputs. It is not economically possible to have prosperous farmers at the State expense and low prices for food.

The Romanian case is highly significant. Considering that the official statistics are correct, 40% of the active population works in agriculture. Economically, the remaining 60% active population working in other sectors cannot support them. If the proportion had been 10/90, things would have been quite different.

Romanian farming produces are not competitive on foreign markets. However, their prices on the domestic market are lower than those in the West. Otherwise, the rest of the population, poor as it is, could not buy the bare food necessities. The small prices on the Romanian market can be maintained only by selling the produces at a loss. This is possible because the workforce in agriculture in underpaid. The farmers consider everything: tilling the land, seeds, fertilizers maybe, cropping, except their work. They are satisfied if they can cover their expenses. How much is the workforce worth? Nobody knows. It just ensures the survival of the farmer and of his family.

30.12. The problem of the Romanian agriculture is the Romanian industry

The Romanian agriculture will never develop with the resources it creates until industry has stopped subduing it. "Agriculture saves Romania" is just a fairy-tale because agriculture will never be able to develop with the burden of an inefficient industry. However, supposing industry is restructured, for at least a decade from no on, it will not be able to absorb workforce. Therefore, not only agriculture, but industry as well will have too much workforce and major social problems will arise.

Romania cannot avoid these atypical problems; the only solution is to reorganize industry so that agriculture can use its own resources at least.

Another aspect is related to Romania trying to become a member of the European Union. The issue is rather complex and it is not at all debated in Romania. Romania should not commit itself until the fate of agriculture, one of the few fields with good prospects here, has been considered.

The problems are complex. European Union exports farm products and has no interest whatsoever in Romania turning to good account its agricultural potential.

Therefore, Romania has to decide if the possible advantages it could get indirectly and on a long term in industry and in other economic sectors compensate for the certain loss of turning to account its agricultural potential. Unfortunately, agriculture will be inhibited during the preliminary stages of negotiations whereas Romania's integration into the European Union is just a project considering the very high standards it has to reach.

CHAPTER 31

Poor or rich budget?

Similarly to other economic fields, the disastrous post-December budgets bore the unmistakable signature of Petre Roman government. On the one hand, the improper and useless populism at the beginning of 1990 rapidly stretched both the budget and the currency reserve to their limits. On the other hand, the dissociation of the public authority-State from the owner-State, in principle a correct movement, proved to be totally destabilizing due to the specially created confusions.

The State budget thus became the budget of the public authority-State, fed by taxes, whereas the owner-State budget fed by the benefits of the State enterprises stopped being an object of public report. State enterprises became autonomous and the State stopped asserting its power in managing them. Practically, nobody owned them and that explains the accumulation of losses and arrears: the successful companies kept their profits whereas the non-performing ones kept on "nationalizing" their losses (credit losses were "nationalized"). However, the balance was not made between profitable and non-profitable companies but at the expense of the public-authority budget, that is of the population.

As the budget of the public authority-State was exclusively made of taxes, it soon became one of the poorest in the world. As the taxes inherited from communism were low, Romania started its way to market economy with a huge handicap. Petre Roman government kept forcing the budget to support price subsidies for staples products and services and consequently taxation increased.

In the absence of a national economic project, no strategy was conceived for the role of the State budget. The budgetary philosophy remained unchanged. This ossification proved extremely harmful although, within the general improvisation and dissolution, the budgetary inertia seemed a pillar of stability.

The taxation increase did not much help the State budget to honor its basic mission. The Romanian political class constantly subjected it to unprecedented aggression. Budget thus became the source for filling the gaps generated by incompetence, imprudence, or simply by thefts.

31.1. A permanent aggression

Almost unbelievably, the aggressor was not some foreign power but the very political class of Romania. Its representatives generously helped themselves to public money (for their own interests or of the groups they belonged to) and irrespective of their political color they accepted, for political or electoral reasons, the public money to be wasted for objectives it had no connection with.

Gradually, the budget of Romania started being wasted to support loss-generating factories, to cover banks robberies (pompously called "banking system restructuring"), and to keep alive the pensions scheme bankrupted by anticipated retirements instead of unemployment. In such conditions, not much money was left for financing education, health, culture, or national defense.

Immediately after 1989, during the first Iliescu administration, the budget had to support the broken factories that dragged the whole economy down causing the so-called "financial blockage".

Likewise, Petre Roman and Vacaroiu governments and then RDC-DP administration forced the workers in uneconomic factories to retire earlier instead of idling them.

As the pension scheme was broken, they turned to the State budget that had no connection with that issue.

Last but not least, the so-called "restructuring" of the banking system stroke the final blow against the budget. Under that demagogical name, the public debt took over a large part of the credits granted to the fake billionaires that never returned them. Therefore, the domestic public debt did not increase because of the budgetary deficit but because of some special normative deeds allowing budget payments. In 2000, those payments represented 35% of the whole domestic public debt.

The budget took over the debts of Agricola Bank and of Bancorex. The Bancorex debt itself represented 40% of the annual budget incomes. In such conditions, is Romania's budget rich or poor? What poor budget could afford to pay for a debt representing almost half of the burden it has anyway.

The officials said that the budget was forced to take over the Bancorex burden because the bank would have otherwise collapsed and would have entailed the collapse of the whole banking system. Consequently, the people's savings would have disappeared and the Romanian economy would have collapsed as well. I doubt that it is true; it is however certain that such a thing would have happened if the other banks had been in a similar situation. Maybe the decision makers know better!

Why was the State budget so severely aggressed? Because those who robbed Bancorex and took 2.5 billion *lei* could thus live in elegant buildings and buy expensive cars! They and those who helped them get cheap money have to be punished. The poor population paid too dearly for that money. The guilty ones have to pay!

Mention should also be made of the "consolidated public budget" – just another instrument for besetting the public money. The Romanian officials tried to avoid an open increase of taxes by inventing other taxes meant to form special funds (for developing the power system, for roads, for supporting tourism, for the pensions of the ex-members of the Agricultural Production Cooperatives, etc.). On the other hand, they used the initial budget excess of the national insurance to cover State budgetary deficits. Therefore, IMF imposed as a negotiation benchmark, the "consolidated public budget" including all the public incomes and expenditures, so that the governments in Bucharest could no longer avoid their obligations by making all kind of transfers among the State budget, the budget of the national insurances and other special budgets.

The effect of such an enterprise was a positive one, but making up such a "cauldron" meant a "de-individualization" of each segment management and, consequently, the State budget took over the problems of all the other budgets.

However, the most aggressive of all are the companies that do not pay their taxes and duties: 90% State companies and 10% private ones. In fact, the taxes collecting rate is less than 2/3.

Tax evasion in Romania is open and on a large scale.

31.2. Dodgers and goofy good payers

Under the spur of their political and electoral goals, and mainly of the pork-barrel politics in action, the governments have simply irresponsible positions versus such tax evasions. No steps have been made to normalize the situation; quite the contrary, measures are taken to exempt the bad payers from their duties, to spread out those debts, or to reschedule them. Ironically, when the Liberal Party shared power, the liberal parliamentarians made an outrageous attempt to amnesty the bad payers, the private ones included. Obviously, part of the beneficiaries would have been those parliamentarians themselves.

However, exemption and rescheduling are common practices of each government and the arguments are the same: there would be too many jobless, the debts could never be recovered, atypical situations ask for atypical measures, exemption and rescheduling could be the very solution if the bad payers are properly conditioned, etc. Facilities for the so-called historical debts could be granted if the present debts are paid. Thus, the financial blockage favored by the historical debts could be removed and everybody would be happy. Except for the State budget, of course!

Obviously everything is a cock-and-bull story since the most important exemption and rescheduling beneficiaries are not the victims of the financial blockage but those responsible for it. In fact, exemption and rescheduling help them generate even more losses, they go on without paying their suppliers, and gradually more and more are caught in the debtors' chain. Consequently, arrears accumulate and the State budget has no chance to escape.

The system creates a kind of "moral hazard": those who used to pay their taxes are encouraged not to since rescheduling and exemptions are so easily granted.

Complete lack of economic criteria in granting these facilities turns everything into a discretionary and cliental action with negative impact: honest people are a kind of goofs who pay their taxes.

More than that, each serious foreign investor considers that such an attitude could lead to unfair competition and prefers not to come to Romania.

A new budgetary philosophy meant to encourage the economic activity is a must! However, investments and economic activity cannot be stimulated without resources. For the beginning, the necessary resources can only be ensured in two ways: deliberate reversal in the expected order of incomes by increasing property (houses, land, cars) or consumption taxes (VAT, excises) for decreasing production and labor income taxes; or by a strategic ranking of the budgetary expenses for reducing them (*strategic*, by giving up or restricting the budgetary intervention in certain fields).

Another scheme could be significant reduction of the profit taxation percent together with increase of the dividend taxation percent so that the investment profit could be indirectly, but substantially encouraged. The companies could thus take over part of the financial task required for their capitalization. The scheme would include the dividends in the quantum for calculating the income tax: increased dividend taxation would thus be closer to that of the work incomes. Likewise, the foreign companies in Romania would have no interest in hiding their profits by "transfer prices".

31.3. The prohibitive cost of the workplace

A basic component of a budgetary and economic philosophy in Romania would be the significant reduction of the present prohibitive cost of the workplace. This cost reported to the net wage is 1.5–1.8 higher than in the member- or candidate-countries to the European Union.

Romania has got more retired than working people, that is more beneficiaries than contributors to the pension scheme. All the post-December governments are responsible for this situation: instead of idling workplaces, people had to retire. Following 1990, about 3.6 million workplaces were idled but less than 1 million people are officially unemployed. Therefore, nobody should wonder that the contributors-beneficiaries ratio has been dramatically inversed: more than 2.6 million ex-contributors have become beneficiaries.

Obviously such a situation cannot be changed easily. The constraints in the pension scheme have to be economically accepted because the present pensioners are not guilty and cannot be abandoned. However, they should be told, and the politicians refuse to do that, that their pensions will have to decrease in relation to wages.

The constraints are huge and no others country faces such problems: the financial obligations to be paid for the pension scheme in Romania are about 15% higher than in the most European countries and this difference cannot diminish since the pension scheme survives only on account of the State budget that should have no connection with it.

Romania seems doomed to a vicious circle: the pension scheme absorbs resources to be used for development investments and thus the possibilities to face constraints in the pension schemes, among others, are lower.

The most serious impact is the prohibitive cost of a workplace. The workers contribute one third to the pension scheme and their employers pay the rest. Likewise, the employers pay half of the health insurance and the largest part of the contribution for unemployment and organized activities. Taxes and insurances represent in Romania about 44% of the gross income; the net wage is thus about 56%. However, the main problem is the high cost of the workplace. If the gross income is, let us say 100, the cost of the workplace is 134. Obviously, a very small part of it, in comparison with other countries, is net wage. Therefore, for an average net wage, the workplace costs 2.4 times more. In Spain the ratio is 1.4, in Portugal and Czech Republic 1.5, in Hungary and Poland 1.6, and in Germany 1.7. It is therefore no wonder that such a prohibitive cost encourages black labor and discourages the serious foreign investors who cannot afford to evade law.

Comparison with other European countries shows that all of them have to face the unfavorable change of the beneficiaries-contributors ratio in the pension scheme, mainly because of the population ageing. All these countries dramatically decreased the taxation of the gross wage to avoid more expensive workplaces. In Austria, France, and the Netherlands, which maintain high contributions for insurances and pensions, the percent quota of the income tax is very low (5–10%). In Romania it is 24%.

The level of income taxation in Romania is higher than in other European countries, members of the European Union or just candidates. Low income taxation in other countries is possible because of the higher taxation of fuels (gasoline, derv, and diesel). In Romania, the only country in Europe where pump gasoline costs the equivalent of half a dollar, the wages, the lowest in Europe, are the most heavily taxed.

31.4. Excises on gasoline to reduce wage taxes

If Romania does not increase the gasoline price to $1 it has no chance of development.

The cons are: transportation will collapse; inflation chain will be devastating; there will be no correlation with the wages in Romania.

However, a short analysis shows that none of the above cons is true. Everywhere in the world the fuel taxes are high: they represent 70–80 cents of $1, the price of pump gasoline. However, other countries have good roads because there is no other way to finance infrastructure. It is therefore both natural and correct that those who use roads should pay for them. The goods to be transported will be transported irrespective of the price. In the last years, the transportation activity decreased as a consequence of the decrease in economic activity and not because of fuel price increase. Transportation will certainly be more expensive. However, the impact of that price increase cannot be excessive and it will calm down after the initial shock.

The wage issue is quite different than it seems. The wages are low in Romania because of the poor quality of work productivity. The authorities do not have to correlate the gasoline price and the wages; there are neither economic nor social reasons to do such a thing. Quite the contrary! Economically, high prices encourage power saving and reduce imports. Socially, protection should focus on the poor and not on the wealthy ones. In Romania, gasoline was cheaper because the excise taxes paid for it were lower. Therefore, the budget had to find other sources, mainly from withholding taxes.

Increase in excises on fuels would have a positive role provided that the withholding taxes and subsidizing public transportation for the poor decrease correspondingly. Funds for financing infrastructure could be thus obtained alongside reduction of the workplace costs. Consequently, unemployment and tax evasion will diminish and the increase in domestic demand will no longer be inflationary.

Therefore increase of the excise taxes for pump gasoline to $1 is economically and socially beneficial as a part of the mentioned fiscal reversal only. If such a reversal is not possible, further increase in gasoline excise tax will be simply harmful. The money from higher excises will be used only to fill the gaps created by the unproductive sectors that do not pay their taxes.

31.5. Discrediting the necessary taxation

The total income taxation was crucial in the fiscal reform in Romania. It was introduced on January 1, 2000 and had two goals.

The former goal was social: higher total incomes will be taxed more heavily than the lower ones. Equitable enough! Unfortunately, the scheme excludes three great categories of incomes (interests, dividends, and capital market gains). The explanation that separate taxation, by withholding the source, could ensure better collection is arguable.

In fact, it is not a new taxation system but an additional tax for certain incomes only: wages and independent activities, respectively. Unfortunately, while small wages are taxed 18%–40%, higher incomes, sometimes billions *lei* resulting from dividends, are taxed 5%.

The latter goal was economic: to eliminate tax evasion by surfacing the illegal incomes in the black economy. Certain activities performed within black economy would have benefited from tax deductions similarly to those performed officially. In this way, both employers and employees would have been interested to obey the law.

This kind of taxation is economically efficient, socially equitable, and morally correct. Unfortunately, the way it is applied in Romania is full of flaws.

The incomes already taxed are taxed even more heavily while more important untaxed incomes will remain untaxed. This formula does not envisage any economic scheme for identifying, surfacing, and taxing the latter category of incomes. Obviously, a house painter, a plumber, or a private tutor will never declare their incomes as long as their beneficiaries' expenses for such services are not tax deductible. In this way, unaudited incomes from parallel economy have no chance whatsoever of being surfaced.

Illegal incomes have even fewer chances of being taxed; black economy and its beneficiaries are not affected by the new taxation. The way the total income taxation is applied defies the honest people who toil for their money and complete their income-tax returns. It is just another "gift" for all felonies, it is simply a shame.

In Romania, the total income taxation is rather an additional taxation than a new taxation system. Without major corrections in its very conception, mainly in the field of deductions, this efficient and equitable taxation will be compromised.

31.6. Health insurance – a step forward

The health sector in Romania underwent an essential reform: the so-called national organization, totally financed by the State, was replaced by an insurance system financed mainly by its beneficiaries. Such a reform was expected to produce destabilization and dysfunction, mainly in such a country as Romania where all the sides of economic and social life are institutionally deficient. In other countries, the very high costs of such destabilizations and dysfunctions were absorbed by the national budgets. The costs were not so high in Romania but they were supported by a practically destroyed budget that could not fulfill its own attributions.

Mention should be made that the new organization system collects more money for health than the previous one did. The explanation is simple. The great bad payers did not pay their taxes and health resources were distributed from the national budget after collecting taxes in the health account. In the new system, the health tax has been separated from the other taxes and individualized, so that paying it has become a condition for the access to the health services. Consequently, the bad payers started depositing the money collected for health contributions because otherwise they would have had to face their employees.

The money collected for health has to be directed to the Health Houses, the pillars of the new organization system. However, that money enters the so-called "consolidated budget" that concentrates the whole public incomes and expenses kept in trust by the Ministry of Finance. However, several controversies arise. Who will keep the money? The Ministry of Finance decided that the Treasury should keep the money and offer small interests. Of course, the money should have been taken good care of, mainly following the notorious and tragic experiences underwent by the Romanian banking and financial systems (Bancorex or NIF).

Besides the small interests, there was another controversial aspect: the Ministry of Finance, the trustee of the "consolidated budget", refused to unfreeze the money of the Health Houses. The government simply decided to use part of that money for filling some gaps in the public and pension budgets and for financing the so-called "social diseases" – a branch that had remained the responsibility of the public budget. More than that, the funds were used to exempt or reschedule the payments of some organizations that did not deposit the money they had collected for health. Such an intrusion is simply intolerable because that money did not belong to the government and it had no jurisdiction over those funds.

On the other hand, the Health Houses used the money to get expensive premises, extraordinary infrastructures, and luxury cars. The family doctors tried to win as much as possible by inflating their medical services and the hospitals used the opportunity to update their equipments and to increase the wages of their staffs. Finally, no money was left to pay for medicines!

31.7. A new budgetary philosophy

The best solution is to gradually take the insurance systems, the health one included, out of the communist-type "consolidated budget". The past errors should turn into good lessons for the future. For long years the pension budget surplus financed the deficits in the public budget. Now, the roles are reversed and the pension budget is supported by the public one. The health insurance budget wants to be independent. In fact, the surplus of the health insurance budget used by the public budget is equal to the amount the pension insurance budget uses from the State budget!

This vicious circle shows in fact how harmful this communist habit of taking from one part to "mend" other parts is. Instead of being idled, people were forced to retire and before long the pension system overburdened the public budget that became a menace for the health budget.

The success of collecting the health taxes shows the way to be followed by the fiscal reform in Romania: the best payer is the one interested to pay. All health taxes should be paid by the possible beneficiaries of the health services from their own wages. The same should happen with the unemployment benefits. The taxes for social insurance have to be entirely paid by the employees from their wages. Of course, such a change has to be accompanied by increase of the gross wages and by accommodation of taxation so that net wages and workplace costs remain the same. Some inherent problems will arise but they have to be accepted because, on a long term, this is the only solution to eliminate the bad paying employers. If they are able to pay good salaries so that their employees may pay taxes for pensions, health, and possible unemployment they will remain on the market. Otherwise, they will be removed.

31.8. The need of a small budgetary deficit

There is a rather strong perception that increase of the budgetary deficit could be the solution to get out of constraints and the only obstacle is IMF that invariably prescribes a small budgetary deficit. IMF considers that inflation in a country means serious lack of balance that can be improved only by substantially reducing the expenses of both the population and the State. That is why, according to IMF, a small budgetary deficit, i.e. slightly higher expenses than incomes at the State level, is a must for stopping inflation and for regaining economic balance.

However, there exist in Romania some stronger reasons for a small budgetary deficit than the IMF approach.

At the first sight, everybody seems to benefit from a budgetary deficit. The State meets more economic and social goals than it could afford from the resources received. The State employees could have higher wages and the ministries higher allocations. The savers can win more from buying public issues. For the commercial banks the public issues are ideal investments, practically with no risk for the money collected in their deposits.

However, the facts are quite different. If the State borrows at home, part of the money in the market are collected at its disposal. Both what is "physically" left for financing the real economy and what represents the credit cost, i.e. interest, depend on the amount of money in the market. If the State borrows from the abroad, there is only one problem: costs. However, interests, either domestic or external, are supported by the budget, that is by the tax payers. Therefore, what seems a good thing is in fact not so good!

More than 43 250 billion *lei* of the year 2000 budget were used for interests, representing about 30% of the total expenses, about 36% of the State budget incomes, and 5.5% of GDP. Therefore, even less than 2/3 of incomes could be used for financing the very important economic-social goals; the rest was used for interests. In 2000, expenses were apparently higher than incomes; in fact, the expenses for economic-social goals had to be smaller than incomes, so that interests could be paid. All that happened because of the previous budgetary deficits.

The interests of the debts made on the account of the previous budgetary deficits burden the next year budget and it cannot afford a higher deficit than the previous one. A higher deficit would entail higher loan commitments of the State, at the risk of getting a budget that cannot be financed: the part of the income meant to be used for paying interests could become higher than that meant to cover economic-social expenses.

There are two reasons why Romania cannot afford a higher budgetary deficit than the equivalent of 3% GDP. The former is the money "gyration" at almost breakneck speed in Romania. Therefore, little money exists on the market for financing real economy. Much money on the market means inflation and if the State promotes a high budgetary deficit on such a market it simply empties it of money and leaves nothing for financing real economy. In such conditions, the State only pushes up the interests that affect both economic organizations and private tax payers.

The latter reason: Romania can get external loans for financing an increase in the budgetary deficit at 10–11% rates, meaning that it has to pay back more than 12% (commissions included). In five years, Romania would have to pay back an almost double amount. Even if it used these loans for investments only no activity or business could be so profitable as to compensate for such a cost and to ensure the return of the money.

In its honeymoon period, Nastase government did not realize how important small budgetary deficits were for Romania. They tried to make investments starting from a high budgetary deficit. There is that idea that a budgetary deficit has to be small only when the difference between incomes and expenses is used for financing consumption. When the money is used for investments, the budgetary deficit could be higher because the money is returned. IMF that supports the idea of a small budgetary deficit did not agree with Nastase approach. The IMF experts motivate that long-term investments will bring money after long years and the Romanian budget has to got a small deficit at present. Therefore, the stand-by agreement was concluded with a 3% GDP deficit and the investment allocations were limited. Romania's specific situation imposes a very small budgetary deficit, tending to zero.

CHAPTER 32

Who is responsible for the Romanian capital being out of game?

In 1999, the Romanian officials together with IMF and with the World Bank discovered a generally acknowledged fact: the credit losses (the so-called "non-performing credits") suffocated the Romanian banking system. All those credits were in fact loans granted by the State banks to the unproductive State sectors in industry, agriculture, and in other branches, with no chance of being ever paid back; they were also credits granted mainly by the State banks to the post-December billionaires that were never returned. Everybody seemed surprised by such a situation as if the two main private banks in Romania had not been bankrupted four years before by the very same non-performing credits granted to certain customers or to their own stockholders.

Those credits represented, more or less officially, about 30% of the whole credits granted by the Romanian banking system. According to other opinions, they represented more than 50%. It was obvious that if a 30% average was correct, the rottenness in some banks affected 50% of the credits.

Why rottenness? Because the assets of a bank are, besides capital and reserve funds, the credits granted to its customers (the most important part). Liabilities include deposits – money at the customers' disposal. If those who are granted credits do not return the money, the bank comes to a crisis. The Romanian banking system reached such a situation: the interests exceeded significantly the inflation rate and consequently the National Bank tried to counteract a possible "escape" from *leu* to hard currency while the other banks strove after money.

What was then the solution found by the Romanian government, World Bank, and IMF? The public debts should take over the rottenness in the State banks! Concretely, they had to take over the non-performing credits from Agricola Bank and from Bancorex.

Should or should not Bancorex receive budget money? This issue divided the members of the Parliament. It was simply terrifying to force the poor population fill the huge gaps produced in the bank by the non-performing economic sectors and by the private specialists in financial engineering. At the same time, the bank bankruptcy would have meant the bankruptcies of its tens of thousands deponents that had deposited there more than 7 000 billion *lei* (about $ 1 billion) and also a fall of the whole Romanian banking system. Finally, they chose the solution of covering the gaps with budget money. The action was in name only, to prevent destabilization of the whole banking system and mainly to hide the political involvement in the monumental swindles at Bancorex.

32.1. Bancorex – the emblem of the post-December history

Why did Bancorex reach a blind alley? The answer might be very interesting since the Bancorex history mirrors Romania's history in the post-December years.

The bank had inherited the monopoly of financial operations abroad from the command economy. The Romanian Bank for Foreign Trade (RBFT), later called Bancorex, used to advise any foreign financial operation in communist Romania: export returns, import payments, contracting foreign credits, Securitate's secret accounts, and maybe Ceausescu's accounts. Romania's currency reserves were also deposited there. In December 1989, RBFT had about $2 billion and the first post-

December administration led by Iliescu–Roman team quickly spent them on useless imports and on populist actions that proved to have disastrous consequences on the economic development. Likewise, the first nouveau riches of the transition took advantage of the confusion created and of the legal void to copiously help them to that money.

In the summer of 1990, the $2 billion had already vanished. In 1991, when the National Bank was established as a central bank, having the role of issuing money, monitoring the banking system, and storing Romania's currency reserve, it inherited from RBFT very small currency reserves and a gap of more than half a billion dollars, representing foreign commitments in the name of the State that had not been honored.

Petre Roman government partially liberalized prices without liberalizing interests and exchange rate. An unbelievably nonprofessional practice! RBFT, together with all the other banks (all State-owned) were soon down. As prices increased and interests remained within imposed limits, banks remained without capital. Stolojan government was forced to make huge capital transfusions in 1992 to capitalize them. When Miron Cozma, probably in complicity with the then president of the country, toppled Petre Roman government, the whole Romanian banking system had only $3 million. A ridiculous and embarrassing amount for a country! Stolojan government had to issue a decree for forfeiting the currency. In this way, Romania avoided a defaulted on the payment situation. Both tragic and funny for a country with no external debts!

Helped by State contributions, by the currency resources from exports, and by external financing, RBFT succeeded in maintaining its leading position in the field of currency operations (although it was no longer a monopoly) based on its previous connections.

Unfortunately, the division of the public "cake" entered a new stage in post-December Romania. At the beginning, the wealth had been taken by armfuls, at random. In the new stage everything was organized following a pork-barrel politics. RBFT became the keystone in the new system and adopted a new name: Bancorex. Bancorex became the king of the great appropriations of funds; it created fake billionaires and supported them. Some of the fake billionaires had managerial abilities and went on with their business, returning part of the money they had borrowed. Some others remained fakes: they bought expensive cars and lived in big houses but did not pay their debts.

The bank and its staff bought their immunity by preferentially lending money to policemen, attorneys, judges, and politicians. They also credited, obeying political orders, bankrupt organizations and financed power imports. Practically, the bank financed the Vacaroiu government policy of stimulating industry before restructuring by forcing the State accounts and Romania's external accounts. Of course, the bank managers did not forget their own accounts!

Bancorex had gone over the top: the non-performing credits represented 75%; 60% of them were recorded in the private sector.

Because of the permanent lack of money it had to face, Bancorex started to generate high interests, much above the inflation rate. The bank borrowed from the bank market at any cost and it gradually contaminated the whole market.

Useless to say that all this pathetic show that lasted several years used only public money and people's savings.

Ciorbea government had to take a decision. However, their decision that the public debt should take over non-performing credits from Bancorex and from Agricola Bank was wrong. Careful analysis of the debits shows that only 2/5 of them were unredeemed credits resulted from the policies imposed by Vacaroiu government: credits for power imports and for the State agriculture, respectively. The rest of 3/5 represented credits granted to private beneficiaries and should not have been taken over by the public debt. Such an action represented in fact a "nationalization" of losses to the benefit of privatizing some small groups' profits.

Although Bancorex was on the verge of bankruptcy, the members of the coalition fought for grasping it; both DP and NPP wanted to milk it for all it still had.

In the meantime, the Bancorex management started to use the fresh money they had received from the budget. Sixty percents of the public securities were immediately sold to get cash. The result was a violent inflation outburst. However, the Bancorex management showed flawless lack of decency when announced profits of 800 billion *lei* at the end of 1997 and tried to push the government into using the money to increase the bank capital.

It was time for the World Bank to take a firm stand then. The restructuring program they had asked in the summer of 1977 became absolute imperative: Bancorex restructuring or no relation with Romania. The political crisis at the beginning of 1998 delayed the World Bank action. However, the World Bank intervention showed both DP and NPP that Bancorex was not a milking cow. DP withdrew and received the management of the Development Bank; NPP was a bad player and received nothing. Although the new bank management idled part of its staff, sold the expensive cars, buildings, etc., Bancorex still needed funds injection to honor its payments.

The final decision was that Bancorex should be absorbed by Romanian Commercial Bank (RCB). The Agency for Valuing Bank Assets (AVBA) took over the non-performing credits for their possible recovery. In fact, by setting up AVBA, both the budget and the population received a dramatic financial blow while the culprits and profiteers of Bancorex and of Agricola Bank became spotless.

32.2 The shame called AVBA

The very idea of setting up AVBA was a shame. The agency was not created just to help banks recover their assets that should have otherwise been registered as bed debts. Some private organization could have solved the issue better than a government agency. In fact, the agency was created to fill in the gaps in the State banks with the population's money. The already poor population was thus forced to clean up the rottenness in the banks whereas nobody was made responsible for granting non-performing credits: neither the bank managers nor the politicians who commanded fund appropriations or waiving the debts of the bankrupt organizations.

Why should have the agency had more chances of recovering the non-performing credits than the banks themselves? Who could have believed such a thing since the government could not recover its money from the organizations that had not paid their taxes and their national insurance contributions? Likewise, what was the use of a State representative to recover some debts that belonged to the shareholder-State represented by SPF at that time?

AVBA recovered a ridiculously small part of the banking assets in its management and at very low prices (2–3 times lower than those accounted for when the organization as set up). In fact, AVBA reached the goal it had been set up for: it sank into oblivion the rottenness in the State banks.

32.3. The only solution: to attract well-known western banks

The examples of Bancorex and Agricola Bank showed that privatization was the only solution to avoid the unwelcome and harmful intrusion of politics into banks. In fact, privatization is not a solution in itself since so many private banks had the same fate as the ones mentioned above. The Romanian market should attract some western banks that have a name and a public image to protect.

Taking over of the Romanian banking system by such banks, privatizations included, is a must, the only solution for rebuilding the seriously affected credibility of the banking system. Likewise, the perception on the banks property has to change. Although the management and not the shareholding structure is essential in banks – so that they should be privatized by increasing their capitals and not by direct acquisition – the idea of the strategic investor in banks had to be accepted as the only way of permitting preponderant takeovers by famous western banks. Therefore, the first bank was not privatized by increasing the capital but by taking it over by a strategic investor: the Romanian Bank for Development (RBD) was taken over by the French group Société Générale.

The moment was crucial for the Romanian reform: a new cycle of implications was triggered for placing, sooner or later, the whole economic circuit within market criteria.

In such conditions the relatively small price $ 200 million got for the controlling interests of RBD was not very important.

Although banks should keep their public character and have an as much as possible depersonalized capital, there is no alternative for Romania: banks should be taken over by strategic investors, the only ones able to impose the market rules on the Romanian market and the prudence ones for the banking system.

The several-year delay in the privatization of the first bank cost Romania very much. (The same happened in the case of Romtelecom). On the one hand, the cycle of implications mentioned above was triggered too late and, on the other hand, the price RBD received was 2–3 times smaller because the trusts of the foreign investors had been altered in the meantime by the Asian crisis and by the financial collapse in Russia.

To accept privatization by strategic investors meant to assume the gradual loss of the Romanian character of the banking system since the only private strategic investors could be foreign banking groups. However, Romania was left with no other alternative. It has to pay for the unprofessional and imprudent management in the Romanian banks, for political intrusions, and for the huge thefts in the State banks that shattered the Romanians' confidence in them. The story of Agricola Bank, that had a happy end, is eloquent for a privatization with population's money.

The unwise policy of the first PSDR administration – the National Bank was forced to issue money to subside the bankrupt State agriculture – rapidly caused Agricola Bank collapse. The bank soon became insolvent under the burden of the "non-performing credits". Instead of winding up the broken bank and covering the deponents' savings, the RDC administration went on with the same mistakes as the previous one maybe in the unrealistic hope of privatizing it: the public debt took over the "non-performing credits" meaning that the population had to pay $700–800 billion. However, nobody wanted to buy it without having been recapitalized first. Who was to recapitalize it? The population, of course!

Mugur Isarescu used to say that Romania had to sell the furniture in its house to get around the difficult situation. The role of privatization to foreign investors was thus rather suggestively exemplified. It is not very honorable but it is understandable to sell the furniture when you are poor. But to give money to have your furniture taken away is an extravagance a poor people cannot afford. Unfortunately that was the case of Agricola Bank.

Finally, Agricola Bank was privatized for $ 15 million after the Romanian taxpayers had paid $1 billion for keeping it afloat. The buyer – a consortium made up of the Romanian-American Investment Fund and the Raiffeisen Austrian banking group – pledged to capitalize immediately the bank with $37 million. However, the Agricola Bank privatization was of good omen for at least three reasons.

First, the bank was saved. Therefore, the State expensive financial interventions for saving it were not finally useless.

Second, the wide banking network could be maintained owing to fresh capital infusion.

Third, the investors offered the necessary credibility for refloating the bank. The Romanian-American Investment Fund is known for its non-spectacular, but very rigorous and successful financial involvements. The Raiffeisen Austrian banking group covers almost a quarter of the market in Austria and is very dynamic in Eastern and Central Europe. Maybe the most important thing is that the 130-old Austrian group has developed the segment of working with the population. The involvement in this segment activity is essential since it is the only one that can ensure efficient restructuring and credibility of the banking system.

Agricola Bank was the second bank took over by a foreign bank. The success of RBD in attracting population's deposits and the credits of the economic organizations unequivocally proved how important it was for the Romanian banks to be backed by strong and reliable banking groups. These good examples should be followed by the Romanian Commercial Bank that should be taken over by a strong and famous western group, able to manage one third of the Romanian banking system. Otherwise, it should not be privatized. Romania can no longer afford experiences of the Romtelecom kind or of the so-called "Romanian-Turkish Bank" type with dubious reputation (one of its vice-presidents was trying to smuggle through customs money hidden in his briefcase).

Romania should obtain from the World Bank the termination of the PSAL agreement for privatizing CEC. The reasons are obvious. Any private owner would immediately liquidate, out of profitability reasons, almost half of the CEC network. However, that network has to be maintained since it is almost the only safety one at the disposal of millions of Romanians, mainly of those living in villages. That is why, CEC has to keep its structure for a while and be what it was set up for: a State savings bank, at the population's disposal, able to offer total guarantees to its deponents, and with investment rights in State securities only.

32.4. The serious responsibilities of the National Bank

When the public debt had taken over the non-performing credits of Bancorex and Agricola Bank, the disaster in the Romanian banking system reached its climax. The National Bank was made responsible for such a disaster since it accepted with no comment the political commands irrespective of their color.

The National Bank knew what was going on inside Bancorex and accepted not to monitor it since politically it had no practical jurisdiction there. Likewise, the National Bank accepted to free money for the State agriculture, although a central bank had other things to do.

The National Bank is also guilty of covering up the greatest theft in the post-December times: the $400 million robbed from Dacia Felix Bank. This money was taken from the National Bank itself by the overdraft mechanism and the Bank did not protest for several months out of political reasons.

The National Bank is responsible for the chain bankruptcies of Bancoop, Albina Bank, International Bank of Religions, and of the Romanian Bank of Discount because it did not monitor them and because, out of political reasons as well, it tolerated the state of things there for too long.

In none of these cases did the National Bank warn in due time about the illegal activities and not a single resignation attempt was made to force the political intrusion stop.

If Mr. Isarescu, the head of the National Bank, had tendered his resignation in one of these circumstances, with the precise and official motivation that the political intrusion should stop, and his successor had done the same thing the situation in the Romanian banking system might have been quite different now.

32.5. Well groomed with population's money

At the beginning of 2000, the National Bank made public the report on the improved situation in the Romanian banking sector, but it did not say a word about either the reasons that had caused the previous disaster or the way the system was saved with population's money.

According to that report, the Romanian banking system was in 2000 much healthier than in the previous years. However, the report was not transparent enough in explaining such a change. The true explanations were hidden behind some euphemistic technical-financial formulas such as stricter supply, less non-performing credits, etc.

However, the explanation was very simple: the population had to pay for all the lawlessness in the banks through the State budget, the final stage of a scenario in which those responsible for administering the public money acted from expedience, not from principle. Sequence 1: the credits were either wasted on non-economic activities or on expensive buildings, luxury cars or deposits abroad. Sequence 2: the respective banks became insolvent because the money was not given back and the bank was not able to honor its deponents. Sequence 3: lawlessness and political interests protected the really guilty ones, i.e. the officials in the banks who had granted credits. Token investigations started and several names were exposed publicly. Finally, they got away with it since they were not really guilty. Sequence 4: the government officials ascertained the theft and "found out" that they had no choice. If the bank was broken, at least the deponents had to receive their money. Otherwise, the whole banking system would collapse. The alternative was to "compensate" the non-performing credits, namely to force the population to pay them through the budget.

Unfortunately, the system is so devilish that the population has to pay for the bankruptcy of some private banks as well. The managers of those banks do not object to being adjudicated bankrupt. Quite the contrary! They arrange their banks bankruptcies. Following exaggerated publicity and high interests, some private banks are robbed because of non-performing credits made by their stockholders or by their acolytes. The deponents cannot be paid their money and the National Bank makes the bank bankrupt. The shareholders and the managers remain with the money and the deponents are paid by other banks through the guarantee fund set up with this aim in view. The other banks recover their money from the inflation differential funds raised from the population as well. Because of numerous bankruptcies, that fund has been exhausted and the deponents are compensated by a credit from the National Bank that can soon become "non-performing". What is the National Bank? The Romanian State. Such an organization of the guarantee system is simply an invitation to robbery!

Unfortunately, it was only after so many thefts that the National Bank thought of stricter surveillance. One of the main measures against the proliferation of the non-performing credits was stricter provision of the loans: the banks were obliged to write off any credit that was delayed beyond an accepted limit. However, if stricter surveillance means this measure only, the effect might be quite different than expected. The banks will thus be even more discouraged to credit real economy; they will prefer to have no risks and to lend the State only, by purchasing public issues from the National Bank.

Such a tendency is already present. The above-mentioned report of the National Bank showed that the banking system – healthier, more solvent, and more performing as it was – was not more useful! The credits granted were lower in 2000 than in the previous years; those granted to real economy were ridiculous. Therefore, a question arises: why has been the population forced to support the improvement of the banking system? Just to make it better groomed?

32.6. The victory of the Romanian thefts over the Romanian banks

The banking system battens on the advantages offered by the legal obligation of the economic organizations to carry on their business through banks rather than on the economic activity of crediting those organizations. The banks can thus afford both to pay lower interests than the inflation rate and to charge high fees.

The too long domination of anti-economy in the Romanian economy was decisive. After the monetarist recipes imposed the absurdity of almost double interests in relation to inflation, the banks used to finance with no risk, i.e. without lending to the real economy; they simply started to lend to the State by purchasing governmental titles and live off the inflation differential funds that finally came from the population. This is one of the expressions and components of the unhappy separation between the monetary economy and the real economy in Romanian transition. As the banks had got rid of the unorganized economy and obsolete industry they were helpless when the interests decreased drastically following an unprecedented situation in Romania: the monetary policy of the National Bank and the fiscal policy of the government were, for the first time, congruent.

The banks had too much money and they started to push the State to issue titles at convenient interests, namely interests that could ensure the prosperity differential funds. That was why the money seemed to be in excess although it was very little. The ones who needed it could not get it whereas the ones who had money did not use it. This is double anti-economy! While there are not resources for pensions and wages, the army has no food, police has no gasoline, hospitals have no medicines, economic organizations have no credits, the banks have too much money and do not know where to invest them. As a matter of fact there is a general lack of confidence in the Romanian banking system; at the same time, it is separated from the real economy.

These desiderata have to be fulfilled. Unfortunately, they will be the task of a banking system that will be Romanian in name only. The victory of the Romanian thefts over the Romanian banking system has been accomplished! Therefore, the Romanians have to regain their confidence in banks and the banks have to support real economy.

CHAPTER 33

What is the use of a capital market in Romania?

The main element in the capital markets is the confidence or lack of confidence in the shares of a company, the confidence or lack of confidence that lies at the basis of each transaction.

The transactions in the capital market are speculative. This is the reality. The speculation as a function of anticipation is the very object of the transactions in the capital market. In any case, the shares are not purchased for the dividends in themselves but for the possible profits generated by shares going up or down. The share prices may increase when the general confidence in economy or the confidence in a certain company increases. Such a tendency is called bull market.

Long bull markets generate higher share prices than the dividends the companies effectively float for each share. The ratio between the share prices and dividends is an important indicator of the stock market evolution and shows in fact the speculation degree at a certain time. Historically, share prices 20–30 times higher than the dividends floated were generally admitted to be dangerous. However, in the present practice those safe limits were exceeded 70, 80, and even 100 times. Nothing can be more speculative. When too long bull markets lead to self-financing, meaning that the above-mentioned ratio is too high, corrections are made: the share prices decrease to more reasonable levels. The important stock market crashes are in fact violent corrections.

33.1. Stock exchange cannot be better than bad economy

Although the capital market and real economy in a country may have distinct dynamics for longer or shorter periods, the capital market will finally reflect the real state of economy. In fact, the object of the capital market is to collect the available money on the market and to develop economy, as it is the surest vector of investments in economy. Objectively, money directs to the most profitable investments and companies can attract it by new flotation for capital increase only if they are profitable. The key-element of the capital market is confidence. That is why the capital market may be more dynamic than a real economy following a good direction because confidence or lack of confidence can change a lot of things. However, the capital market can never be better than an economy following a bad direction because nobody ever trusts such an economy.

Unfortunately, this is the situation in Romania. Romanian real economy follows a bad direction suffocated as it is by loss- and arrear-generating companies. In the absence of legal measures meant to broke the vicious circle characterizing Romanian economy, this lack of confidence of the Romanians and of foreigners alike is even deeper.

In such conditions, the capital market in Romania has been vegetating but it can become more dynamic provided real economy refloats – a rather remote perspective. In any case, the collapse of the Romanian capital market is not an echo of the crashes on the foreign capital markets. Although such an echo cannot be ignored, the lack of vigor in the Romanian capital market is rooted in real economy.

Capital market attracts buyers because of the higher profits that can be made there: the shares the profitable companies float will be sold better tomorrow and that entails investors' confidence.

Buying and selling shares and other securities represent the stock exchange activity and not its goal. The basic function of a stock exchange is to enable public companies raise capital by selling securities to investors. Obviously, the companies have to be fully transparent: to make public their economic and financial results and their future intentions as well. Likewise, at least part of their capital should be gathered by public offer.

The propensity to supply money in exchange for shares will be influenced by the existence of a market in which money can be sold. For the time being the capital market in Romania cannot offer the possibility to raise money from it, meaning it is not a central market but a secondary one that deals with transferring shares already floated which are not profitable for the economic organizations. Therefore, those organizations have no interest whatsoever in obtaining quotation on the stock market (Bucharest Stock Exchange) or on the unlisted securities market (RASDAQ).

In fact, the very nature of property explains objectively the poor extension of the capital market in Romania. Many sectors of the national economy (mainly the industrial ones) have high percents of State capital. If the State companies want to obtain quotation at the stock market they risk extending the present inefficient institutional paralysis that opposes restructuring. More than that, privatization by raising capital might fail because of the inefficient State companies. However, if a company chooses to be controlled by an owner or by a group of owners, or if it is taken over by a strategic investor that company has to accept losing eligibility for stock exchange quotation.

At present, private capital organizations are both the least eligible and the least interested to be quoted at the stock exchange. The private companies are generally small or medium sized and they cannot be eligible. At the same time, they are not interested in stock exchange quotation since they prefer to raise money more easily by all kind of arrangements "behind closed doors".

It was generally agreed that the unhappy experience of SAFI and NIF gave a deadly blow to the capital market in Romania. However, that is not true since capital market did not even exist then.

SAFI and NIF pretended themselves to be investment funds. However, without a functional and in extension capital market, investment funds are doomed. Their only aim was in fact to swindle credulous persons.

The profits from a mutual fund can be higher than the profits from a bank only if the former is supported by a functional and developing capital market. A mutual fund collects money from the investors who prefer to transfer the decision of investing their money to a specialized organization instead of buying shares themselves. The profits may be smaller but they are surer because the mutual fund invests in several stocks and failures are compensated for. However, if real economy does not develop, capital market does not develop either and consequently the shares cannot offer higher profits than that offered by banks. When the profit offered by a financial organization is much higher than the average one something is wrong and dubious.

Last but not least, in the absence of a functional capital market, mutual funds cannot offer higher profits than banks (where they deposit their money) and cannot have a fluent activity. Mutual funds must not have liquidities: money should be invested in business. However, they should be able to exchange their shares for cash when needed. Such a thing can happen only on a fluent capital market having enough resources. The capital market in Romania is small and has little liquidity. More than that, there is little interest in buying shares.

33.2 Where was the Romanian State?

Unlike SAFI, NIF developed its activity under certain investment funds regulations. Therefore, one should wonder where the Romanian State was when more than 300 000 investors were swindled.

The main villain was the very organization that represented the State: National Commission of Movables (NCM). Capital market is preponderantly a market of private capital. However, the State – the Romanian one in this case – has to monitor the observance of law. Unfortunately, the National Commission of Movables set up for this very purpose did not do its job; quite the contrary the people there broke the law and they should be made responsible for that.

The NCM regulations were ambiguous and generated interpretations although SAFI had been a sufficient argument for strict and clear regulations. More than that, NCM did not even ask NIF to respect the regulations in force. So, NIF used luring and deceitful television blitz for the investment risks instead of being forced to warn the investors against the entire risks they should take. In order to wash its hands of all responsibility, NCM transferred its obligation to supervise NIF's publicity to an organization set up by the investments funds themselves: the National Union of the Collective Investment Bodies managed by the same Ioana Vlas who managed NIF. Therefore, Ioana Vlas approved its own media-hyped publicity for NIF.

Likewise, NCM accepted NFI to lure its investors with promises of unrealistic returns, more than double as compared with those on the monetary market. NCM knew better than anyone else that these promises were pure mirages because a poor and non-fluent capital market, not supported by a real and successful economy, might not offer higher profits than banks. Since the then managers of NCM did nothing to stop NFI they could be suspected of interested attitudes and should be investigated.

NCM also accepted NIF to function without a bank of deposit, provided as an obligation in the law of the investment funds, i.e. as an additional security for the investors.

NCM gave up the prudential regulations and permitted NIF risky investments, such as the so-called "unquoted shares", namely shares of companies that were not included in the unlisted securities market (RASDAQ) and used to represent more than 40% of NIF investments. Therefore, there is no wonder that NIF had not the necessary resources to honor the redemption requests.

NCM remained silent when NIF used CEC to offer guarantees to the investors. Even if the irresponsible and maybe interested Camenco Petrovici, the then CEC president, involved his organization in the dubious affair of NIF, both as a Fund investor and stockholder in SOVINVEST (the society for the NIF management) and also as a possible guarantor, there should have existed other national institutions able to penalize such a thing.

How could the National Bank, the representative of the State, tolerate CEC involvement, since CEC should have remained what it was from the very beginning: a saving bank, namely a bank for the population's savings at a national level? What about the Ministry of Finance that was responsible for CEC?

Where were police and magistracy when CEC violated the law? Where was the Romanian State when Ioana Vlas, one of the NIF masterminds, left the country?

One of the most terrifying bits of information was that after one year SRI furnished reports on NFI and on the menace it represented. What did they have to wait so long?

Finally, the State institutions woke up but not to find and punish the guilty ones as expected. The only ones to be punished were the investors who had to finally pay for the damage.

Everything is upside down in Romania. The victims of NIF wanted to recoup their investments from public money, namely from the honest people and not from the thieves who had stolen them. And it was the Justice itself who encouraged those protesting victims to go on with their crazy claims.

When the NIF scandal broke, the Romanian Justice proclaimed that the contract involving CEC was illegal so that they could arrest Camenco Petrovici. After a while, when the protesting NIF victims had already forgotten those who had deceived them, the same Justice proclaimed that the same contract was valid so that the victims might be compensated from public money.

Why were the 6 million CEC depositors guilty to pay for the adventure of more than 300 000 people who wanted rapid and risky profits and were finally deceived by a private financial society? Why did they not deposit their money in CEC where it was protected directly by the Romanian State? They did not do it because the CEC interests were three times lower.

Of course, the NIF victims had a right to try to recover their money. But what connection did they have with the Romanian tax payers? Why did they not try to make Romanian Justice find the guilty ones and make them pay? For the time being, Camenco Petrovici is no longer in jail. However, if the Romanian Justice decides that CEC should recoup for the victims' losses, the 6 million CEC depositors should protest against such an infamy. And if somebody in the government decides that the budget should recoup for those losses, then the millions of tax payers are entitled to call fiscal strike.

CHAPTER 34

The disastrous pension scheme

The new law of pensions put into effect in April 2001 tries to correct at least partly the disaster reached in the pension scheme in Romania.

Ceausescu had left a rather normal situation in the pension scheme and a law ensuring the survival of that scheme. The budget of the national insurance was in excess, so the beneficiaries received their pensions and other supplementary benefits in time. Likewise, the scheme had reserves: more than 3 wages supported one pension. The only menace on a long term could have come from the rather young retirement age if life expectancy had increased.

The disaster came immediately after the events in 1989. The excess inherited from the budget of national insurance was not protected against inflation. Quite the contrary, it was used to cover the deficits in the State budget generated by the harmful policy of subsidizing prices for basic consumer goods although the two budgets had no connection whatsoever.

More than that, a policy started of pensioning off people instead of idling them. In this way, the excess soon vanished and the normal ratio between the contributors and beneficiaries of the pension scheme changed dramatically. Starting with 1996, the pension scheme stopped self-financing. Left with no reserve it had to pay the pensions in one year from the collections of that year only. The contributors-beneficiaries ratio changed drastically: 4.4 million salaried people and 6.2 million retired people. Now, a wage has to support one pension and a half. Despite this disastrous ration, in 1997–2000, the pensions were even higher than wages, a fact that deepened the disaster and created a serious inequality:

people pensioned off in absolutely identical conditions, but in different periods of time, have totally discrepant pensions.

Instead of trying to solve the problem, the NPP-NLP-DP government found a kind of substitute: increase of the national insurance contribution that reached 30%, 35%, or 40% as a function of the category of the working conditions. Such a contribution increased the extremely high price of the working place and explains the huge tax evasion by black labor but also within State companies. A vicious circle, indeed.

For several long years the pension scheme survived only through the State budget, poor as it was. In 2000, the pension budget used more than 4% of the State budget resources although the two budgets had no connection whatsoever.

The new pension law tries to sort things out a little. First of all, it tries to reduce the number of the pensioners by increasing the retirement age: 65 years for men and 60 for women. Out of electoral reasons the gradual increase of the retirement age is very slow, i.e. 14 years, so the short-time effects are almost insignificant. Likewise, the 5-year difference between men and women is rather strange since the life expectancy is higher for women than for men (5 years) in Romania. Such a difference would allow women to benefit from their pensions for almost 15 years whereas men would benefit from theirs only 4 years. However, the new scheme is better than the previous one and will eventually reduce the number of retired people.

The new pension law introduces the long expected equity in calculating pensions as a function of contributions, irrespective of the moment of retirement. Consequently, the pension is linked to the whole contributions made during the claimant's working life and not to certain intervals only chosen by the claimant. The too high discrepancies among pensions may be thus be eliminated.

Thus, the score is recorded of the monthly ratio between the claimant's wage and the national average gross wage. The monthly ratios calculated in this way are used to calculate, for each claimant, the yearly ratios and, based on them, the final score for the whole working life. In this way the calculating base is uniform and the unfair disparities disappear. For the quantum in *lei*, the individual final score is multiplied yearly by the value in *lei* of a pension point that is established by the law of the national insurance budget each year. In this way, the pensions are permanently related to inflation but also to the real possibilities of the pension budget. Better possibilities increase the value of the pension point and therefore pensions themselves; on the other hand, a lower value of the point would entail lower pensions. However, relative decrease of these values avoids dangerous tensions in the pension scheme and consequently delays in payments.

Likewise, the contribution to national insurance is leveled off at an individual wage three times higher than the national average wage. Such a provision, included in all the western pension schemes, is compulsory in a market economy with extremely discrepant incomes. Those having high incomes may use alternative insurance systems to avoid destabilization of the national pension scheme. According to that regulation, the maximum individual score cannot exceed the maximum score allowed, and therefore the highest pension can only exceed three times the quantum of an average pension.

The principle of linking pension to contribution is also reflected in the provision according to which the pension right is only recognized to a highest proportion of one third when the contribution is not paid; the third represents the employee's contribution. The other two thirds will be paid by the employer (unlike the previous law, when the employer paid the whole contribution). However, the regulation is controversial: if the employer does not pay, the employee, who has no guilt at all, has to suffer the consequences. Under trade unions' pressure, this provision is applied only in case of anticipated retirement; otherwise, the rights are integral irrespective of the effective payments of the ex-employers.

The above provisions were put into operation on April 1, 2002. The older pensions have to be re-correlated: the scores of all the pensioners' working lives should be recalculated and the small pensions should increase. If the pensions are higher, there should be no increase until they have reached the quantum stipulated by the new regulations.

As the most pensions in Romania are smaller than they should be according to the new calculation scheme, additional resources should be provided to correlate them. However, the poor budget has not such resources and the re-correlation action will last several years.

The pension system in Romania is in irremediable crisis and it can only survive if the real average pension decreases. It only lives on the contributions of the State budget that has its own more and more stringent problems.

According to some opinions, the so-called "universal" pension funds could be the solution. These funds would be gathered by compulsory contributions of 5%–10% of the wages that should be deduced from the contribution to the national pension scheme. The contributors to these funds should be the employees with more than 20-year-long working lives and, optionally, those having 10–20-year-long working lives.

These funds should be administered by private companies that have to invest the money most profitably and thus to guarantee the pensions of the future claimers.

Private pension funds would represent the most important business in Romania in the decades to come. Until then some of the greatest insurance companies have entered Romanian market: Allianz, AIG, ING Nederlanden, Generali, etc. The universal pension funds could both collect the greatest savings and be the most important investment source in Romania.

However, there is one clear and indispensable condition: the funds should be strictly regulated and State controlled.

It is not clear yet how the massive decrease in the national pension budget could be financed when part of the present contributions will be directed to those pension funds. Of course, an international credit could be borrowed from abroad. Of course, the population will return it directly or not. Is it worth doing such a thing? What capital market in Romania could ensure gains for the portfolio investments made by the pension funds? If the capital market cannot offer such gains everything becomes a failure and the population will have to pay for it; or an indirect gift to the foreign companies that will obviously take over the management of the "universal" pension funds.

However, the regulation of the pension funds should take into account all the recent crises: hundreds of thousands people lost all the money they had long saved. Pension funds gather the money of millions of people: the law should protect them and the serenity of their old ages. These funds must not have the fate of the tragic experiences of such mutual funds as NIF.

CHAPTER 35

Bankrupt social services

A working person and 2.5 people benefiting from social services! A dramatic situation reached in Romania following the demagogical policy of social spending, deeply harmful and economically devastating. All the post-December governments, irrespective of their color, seemed to compete in flaunting their social spending without taking into account either the existing resources or the demands of the market economy. Unlike command economy, egalitarian distribution does not comply with market economy and social services and welfare should be directed to the poor ones exclusively. However, the social spending depends on the general economic development and any attempt to promote a social welfare of the command economy-type is doomed. Unfortunately, this is the case of Romania.

For long years, social services and welfare were identical to the communist ones: the loss-generating economic organizations continued their activity although closing down workplaces should have been more economical; people were not idled but forced to retire earlier; some basic consumer goods and services were generally subsidized instead of being subsidized for the poor only; all the children got allocations instead of the poor ones only; etc. All this and other conjectural social spending connected to varied political interests gradually compromised the chances of building up genuine social services in Romania. More exactly, before starting an operational system its foundation had already been bankrupt.

The social component, the slogan of the post-December policy, was in fact a slightly changed continuation of the social services and welfare characterizing command economy. The main idea was to close down the unemployment safety valve in the name of social supportability. The direct consequence was inflation.

In such conditions, social welfare practically became impossible: there was protection against unemployment but nothing was done in case of inflation. Any mechanism trying to compensate for the inflation effects fed up, in a vicious circle, inflation itself.

Indexation system is an inflationist mechanism in itself. In order to avoid high inflation, the compensation granted should be 50–70% of the forecast raise in the level of prices. A higher compensation means that any further raise in wages, above the forecast one, pushes up inflation. In fact, indexation should decrease the real salary to stop inflation. That happened in Romania. More than that, indexation – no matter how many differentiating levels it has – is a linear system: it does not necessarily protect the poor.

In fact, there are two reasons why no real social services and welfare can be implemented in Romania. Both of them are rooted in the system having its unemployment valve closed up.

First, it is only the monopolist organizations that can benefit from the system because they can impose the prices they want so that their employees can get higher wages than the economic possibilities.

Second, in the respective system, the society maintains bankrupt sectors. Since society spends about 11–12% of GDP to maintain bankrupt industries, economic performance is blocked up and the chance of redistributing additional resources to the really poor ones is low since such resources are absent. Therefore, the little left is rather distributed to the favored ones instead of being directed to those unemployed, disabled, or with small wages.

A ratio of 25 assisted persons to 10 working persons is not sustainable. In such a case there are only two possibilities left: either everything ends up in collapse or the abominable ratio is diminished, mainly by offering social security to the poor only.

The most important contribution to this state of things belongs to Iliescu-Roman team during 1990–1991. Out of ideological, political, and electoral reasons they practically laid the foundation of all the future misfortunes in the social services and welfare by their shameless populism and economic non-professionalism. Mr. Roman's pretence that his government was both "reformist" and ensured the highest living standard in the post-December times was rather outrageous if one considers the economic disaster he initiated. Behind a false and harmful social security, he inaugurated the policy of retirements in advance. The pension scheme received then a severe blow and it will probably never recover again. In the name of a false social security, the largest action directed against market economy started in the same period: a feather-bedding politics was encouraged in loss generating companies using public money. The resources Ceausescu had intended to use for investments were converted directly into wages: practically economy was left lifeblood and inflation exploded. The government also inaugurated a chain of capitulations to the claims for higher wages made by the very employees working in bankrupt companies that should have been closed down. Their action of subsidizing basic consumer goods and services instead of the people most affected by poverty was similarly harmful. In this way, the budget was seriously reduced and four subsequent governments struggled for eight years to make up for it.

Although Vacaroiu government was the most blamed of all for blocking economic reforms, it stopped, in fact, the absurd system of linearly subsidizing food prices and released the budget of the burden it could no longer cope with. Unfortunately it had not the courage to do the same with domestic energy and rents. However, the most serious damage that could be imputed to the first PSDR government was the engineering and implementation of a system for subsidizing non-performing activities that preferred inflation to unemployment. The price paid was at least double. Those benefiting from it blocked the economic restructuring and competitiveness whereas those seriously in need were ignored. Unfortunately, Vacaroiu government continued the policy "better retired than unemployed" that gradually pushed the pension scheme to bankruptcy.

Unfortunately, RDC-DP governments continued the same policy. The Peasant Party promoted non-taxation of the farmlands, a populist measure that discouraged performance in agriculture and placed it in obsolescence. Ciorbea government succeeded an almost impossible thing: to dislocate tens of thousands miners by severance pays and collective redundancies. However, the unhappy generalization of such severance pays changed the Romanian redundant worker into an expensive unemployed, more often than not unwilling to work again. Therefore, the severance pays became a burden for the budget and throttled the labor market. In fact the investment funds for creating jobs were siphoned off.

It was under the RDC-DP governments that a sad record was broken: less than 4.5 million working people had to support more than 6 million pensioners. Out of the former, at least one million were socially protected because they worked in loss-generating companies. If the one million unemployed is added, one can easily see that no economy, no matter how strong it is, can support such social services.

The welfare State the Romanian politicians wanted to turn Romania into is ready to explode Therefore, the government has to adopt urgent measures such as: to limit social spending to the really poor people and to slow down the rhythm of retirement.

Social services and welfare have to be tailored to the resources the Romanian economy can provide; they have to observe the rules of market economy and not a linear assistance that only deepens economic inefficiency. Concomitantly, new jobs must be created so that the ratio between working people and those benefiting from social services stop deteriorating even more. If funds are not reconverted from a passive protection to an active one, social services in Romania have to be adjudged bankrupt.

CHAPTER 36

Exports and moderate payment capacity

While Romania is said to be a market having 22–23 million consumers, it is actually a market of $14 – 14.5 billion representing the yearly maximum payment capacity.

Generally, based on the data at the end of the previous decade (with special reference to 2000), the situation in the external accounts of Romania was the following: in its *current account* about $13–14 billion circulated and in the *financial and capital account* about $ 3.5–4.5 billion. Exports of consumer goods and services represent about $12 billion, transfers (mainly money gained abroad) $1 billion, and capital entries that do not create external debts (investments), $ 1–1.5 billion. The total of $ 14–14.5 represents the yearly payment maximum capacity of Romania.

Also generally, $ 14 billion of that sum are spent on imports of goods and services; $0.5 billion are used for paying interests for the external debt credits.

The rest of $1.5–2 billion of the financial and capital account represents gross movements (entries and reimbursements) of external credits. In 1999, the payments abroad were not compensated by new entries and consequently the National Bank reserve decreased. In 2000, the new entries exceeded by about $1 billion the reimbursements and the National Bank reserve increased.

Therefore, the payments for importing good and services, for repatriation of profits from foreign investments, and for interests of external credits must not exceed this rather low amount of $14–14.5 billion. Any additional capacity that may come from external credits is transient and deceitful, as it supposes both reimbursements and net costs (interests) that affect the import potential for goods and services.

The moderate payment capacity of Romania is finally determined by the low level of exports of the Romanian economy.

A genuine mirror of economy, exports reflect the crises Romania has to face after two decades characterized by the absence of a deep and wide restructuring. Exclusively directed to consuming energy and outdated branches, and based on giant units, Romanian industry has got a huge inertial fund and it is not likely to change. Therefore, the only direction the present Romanian industry can follow is to an inexorable decline. On the one hand its products have increasingly narrower markets; on the other hand, it consumes a lot of energy (more often than not imported). As it cannot finance its own restructuring, the Romanian industry cannot survive in the aggressive international economic competition.

Romanian export offer is that at the level of the 1970s. It is a fallacy that Ceausescu's Romania paid its external debts by forcing exports. In fact, it simply suffocated imports at unimaginable levels. It is not better now. Fossilized in a structure that reflects the structure of national economy, Romanian exports have practically no chance whatsoever. The same companies have been exporting for long years the same products and they have not the wherewithal to revamp; this explains the immobility and the low level of the Romanian exports, record breakers for being the fewest in Europe per capita.

Therefore it is completely false to say that the Romanian exports are low because the State does not subsidize them. In fact, the State, or better to say the population, pays for the losses of the companies exporting products in a system of hidden subsidization; they pay neither their suppliers nor their taxes.

The post-December years changed the exports structure and they have to be judged both qualitatively and quantitatively. If

1993 is taken as a reference, when economy and commerce recovered a little after the terrible shock caused by losing ex-COMECOM markets, some structural tendencies can be noticed.

First, the exports of mechanic and electrical equipments increased from 9% in 1993 to 14% in 2000.

Second, the mineral products (fuels, oils, etc.) decreased from about 12% to about 8% in 2000. The exports of oil products (mainly primary derivatives obtained by refining imported crude oil) were inherited from communist times and represented the worst business possible from the financial point of view. Therefore, their reduction is beneficial. Unfortunately, these exports increased again after 2000 although they had been less than 6% in 1999.

Other two tendencies – decrease in chemical products and commune metals, respectively – should have been strictly positive provided they had been accompanied by increase of the exports in plastics and in processed metal products.

However, all this only affected the exports structure with 10 percent points.

The rest of them were "bad" tendencies: increase in raw wood exports, severe decrease of the exports in furniture, transportation vehicles, or farming produces. These affected the export structures with more than 12 percent points.

Generally, I can say that before 1989 Romania had a more modern export structure than nowadays. At least quantitatively. Qualitatively, mentioned should be made of the absolutely remarkable achievement of directing the greatest amount of exports from East-European and Asian markets to the West-European ones.

Unfortunately, such a change in direction was obtained almost exclusively by the "non-modern" component of exports, a fact that deepened Romania's condition of a peripheral economy.

The present structure of exports cannot solve the problems of the Romanian economy. While most Romanian products are bad and expensive nobody needs restructuring to make them better and cheaper. The only thing everybody asks for is facilities!

Relatively important facilities were granted in 2000 among which privileged taxation (5% instead of 25% in general) of the profits from exports. Consequently, exports increased from $8 – 8.5 billion yearly to more than $10.3 billion. Was that increase due to some transient favorable conditions or did something happen in the production structure?

The statistics show that of the more than $1.8 billion additional exports in 2000 in comparison with 1999, at least 2/3 came from barely processed or unprocessed products, having low VAT, in the textile, footwear, metal, wood, and minerals fields.

Mention should be made of the textile-leather sector where the *lohn* system prevails: foreign companies bring materials and accessories and take then the branded end products to sell them elsewhere. Romania provides workforce. This is the only alternative we have. We like it or not, the cheap Romanian workforce is the only resource we have left.

Estimations for 2000 of the then Ministry of Industry and Commerce showed that 1/5 of the total increase in exports represented workforce export.

However an objective balance should emphasize the employment of the workforce ensured by this system. Unfortunately, the *lohn* system is insecure as the foreign companies are only linked by the Romanian companies by the low wages they pay; any wage increase can make the former leave for other countries where they can find even cheaper workforce.

What about the rest of 4/5 of the exports increase? More than 60% of them are raw materials or half end-products: metals, wood, oil derivatives that gradually exhaust Romania's natural resources. These so-called "bad exports" represented about 50% of the total increase.

The conclusions are not very encouraging.

The facilities granted by Isarescu government had a rather mixed impact. Undoubtedly, they stimulated exports but their general character had, at least in the very case of Romania, two drawbacks. On the one hand they keep supporting the intermediaries instead of helping the makers; on the other hand, they encourage the exports of raw materials – both having disastrous consequences.

Let us see who benefits in fact from these facilities. Statistical data show that more than half of the export activity is achieved in the private sector. Therefore, a serious argument in favor of facilities! What statistics do not show is that more than half of the export returns are taken by private companies. And another thing statistics cannot show is that more than 4/5 of the exported Romanian products are made by the State sector. Who is therefore stimulated by these facilities?

The conclusion is obvious: exports should be supported but the support must be directed to production and mainly to production investment. The present facilities only move money from the poor population's pockets to those of the parasite intermediaries without changing at all the export offer to products that can enter foreign markets on a long term.

If export production is not stimulated, Romania cannot get out of that vicious circle: it can neither be an important market for foreign products nor can foreign investors take advantage of the absorption potential of the 22–23 million

Romanian consumers. This potential has already been compromised by the inability to pay debts caused by the poor exports.

CHAPTER 37

The competitiveness deficit

Actually, the general situation of exports shows a serious competitiveness deficit of economy itself. The Romanian products cannot enter foreign markets and more often than not they have no chance whatsoever on the domestic one either. In such conditions, Romania has to face a massive and difficult to sustain foreign trade deficit.

There is that tendency of the non-performing sector in economy (and of the Romanian nouveaux riches as well) to put its hands further than its sleeves can reach. No matter how much is imported, there is always a "hard core" that keeps consuming energy and raw materials. Therefore economy is permanently beset and indebted by the organizations forming this "hard core". It is also this "hard core" that makes imports insensible to the policies of foreign-exchange rate. However, the most serious effect is that the imports "hard core" substantially absorbs the few resources brought by exports and foreign credits, and thus reduces the acquisitions of modern technologies and equipments. The vicious circle is closed by the Romanian exports incorporating many imports; this explains the existence of a trade deficit when exports are a bit invigorated. In these conditions, the annual imports exceeding exports have rather a negative character: resources are wasted and the domestic consumption has to be supported by excessive foreign indebtedness difficult to be paid back. The gap between imports and exports frequently exceeds the 20% alert quota, thus emphasizing Romania's insecure position in relation to foreign financing.

However, the trade deficit poses two important problems. The former: where does it come from, what generates it? The latter: how is it financed? Obviously, if money does not exist, imports should confine to the export encashment.

The two problems are linked. Its source reveals its tendency and what we could expect. The way of financing shows if we can go on in the same way. The conclusion is devastating. Economically, the deficit tends to increase because of the export and import structures and of the weak competitiveness of the Romanian products as well. Financially, the deficit has to be draconically stopped because there is hardly probable that external money would enter to cover the substantially higher exports. However, the financial argument is stronger than the economic one and Romania will be forced to reduce its imports massively.

Let us see where the trade deficit comes from.

The direct answer is that the Romanian economy is both structurally and technically inefficient and the labor productivity is weak. The same lack of efficiency characterized Romanian economy before 1989 as well but a severe political and economic isolationism protected it then. Now it has to face the aggressive international competition and its lack of efficiency is more obvious than ever.

Starting with 1990, the economy has suffered three shocks generated by the major liberalizations of its relations with other countries. Of course, it is not the liberalizations to be blamed but the fact that nothing has been done to face them.

The liberalization generating the deepest and long-term effects was due to the disbandment of the State monopoly in the field of foreign trade. That meant that any company could export or import everything, anytime, and anywhere. The centre that had distributed import resources and had ensured export markets disappeared. The centralized control of currency also disappeared, although certain restrictions were kept for a while.

However, exports were not able to develop whereas imports rocketed.
In 1990, the deficit was of almost $ 3 billion, although a trade surplus had been recorded in 1989. As the reserves vanished, they were replaced by external resources. As long as these resources were modest, imports exceeded exports within modest limits as well: $1–1.5 billion. The difference increased when a system was devised for using foreign resources on a larger scale. The newly created private economic organizations imported massively and converted their *lei* into hard currency. The State, on the other hand, tried to save its bankrupt companies and borrowed money from abroad to ensure their imports.

The best example is that of Bancorex. For several years, the bank financed power imports in the name of the State, using external loans while the private sector financed its imports of consumer goods by conversions on the currency market. The population had to foot the bill: both the external debts and the gaps left after the bank bankruptcy. Desperate attempts to maintain the *leu* official course had an inauspicious effect: they were an indirect system of subsidizing exports and stimulated the imports of non-profitable activities and non-priority demands.

Disbandment of the State monopoly in the field of foreign trade had strong and long-term consequences because it meant the reconstruction of the whole protection system of the national economy. Unfortunately, the reconstruction was made by ear, without a restructuring strategy. During the communist command economy, the protection of the national economy had been planned: a product was imported only if it had been included in a plan, namely if financial resources had been provided. Market economies protect national economies by customs duties. When the State monopoly stopped operating, Romania had to create customs tariffs that should have worked effectively not in name only as it had happened before. The action was complex and extremely important and should have been included in a long-term strategy for Romania's development. Obviously, the protective tariffs could not meet Romania's demands as the country was involved in a system of international relations where those taxes had been reduced. Therefore, the Romanian producers were gradually sidelined on their own market by more competitive foreign products. Many of them accused protective tariffs to be too high where they should have been low and the other way round. Actually, as nothing had been done to restructure economy effectively, nobody knew for sure if they were right or not.

The scenario repeated itself following the second important liberalization in Romania's foreign trade in 1995 when an association agreement with the European Union was enacted. According to it, a free exchange zone had to exist between Romania and the European Union countries, with no customs tariffs at least in the industrial field. Therefore, the Romanian economy was left with no protection whatsoever in front of the competitive products coming from the West.

Romania had no strategy for preparing its economy, mainly industry, and it did not even know what it wanted during the negotiations. Unfortunately, no measure was taken when the agreement was signed up although it was quite obvious that Romania had to face the strictly predictable consequences of customs "disarmament": invasion of its market with better and sometimes cheaper products from the European Union. In the absence of industrial and economic restructuring measures, the deficit recorded in the relations with the European Union tended to increase although, according to the agreement provisions, the European Union treated more favorable the Romanian products while Romania did not treat the foreign products in the same way. However, this relative advantage tended to fade away with the total customs "disarmament" within the mutual relations. The only exception is the constant trade deficit in Romania's relation with Russia: about $ 1 billion because of the raw material imports, natural gas mainly, and of losing Russian markets.

The lack of competitiveness in Romanian economy manifested itself almost violently following 1997 when the third main liberalization in Romania's foreign trade came up: some reductions in customs duties for food, agreed with the World Bank in the ASAL accord, combined with Romania's stormy integration into CEFTA (Central European Free Trade Area). Food imports simply exploded and some Romanian produces with no tariffs to protect them were simply forced to leave the market. The deficit in the relations with the CEFTA members also exploded because this time the "customs disarmament" was proportional from the very beginning, with no starting advantage for Romania as had happened before.

Obviously, the Romanian economy is not prepared to face the competition generated by such liberalizations and the trade deficit trend to increase can be only limited by the absence of financial resources. How the limitation works is still conjectural: it can be either violent (drop in conversion rate or price explosions) or simple, by stopping imports.

Trade deficit as a chronic manifestation of the lack of efficiency and competitiveness has a major negative impact on a long term and it will influence both the chance of better average wages and the living standard in Romania. Provided that labor productivity increased, the average wage could only reach an international level if exports were stimulated by conversion rate as well. That means that the dollar or euro equivalent of the average wage in Romania cannot increase or can increase very slowly; the present barrier cannot be broken soon and the average net wage cannot be higher than $100 dollars.

CHAPTER 38

Current account: the sword of Damocles

What should we expect from a financial point of view? Or in other words, will Romania have enough resources to finance its further development or at least to keep the deficit within its present limits?

Because of the long communist decades of economic and political isolationism, and of the poor development during the post-December period, Romania has remained outside the international financial circuits. Consequently, the trade relations represent the most important part of the financial flow Romania takes part into. In such a case, its balance of trade is decisive for the external payments as a whole.

38.1. Financing trade deficit

Trade deficit represents more than 90% of the deficit of external current account in the particular situation of goods exchange only. If exports and imports are included, trade deficit is almost every year higher than the deficit of the external current account. Romania is a net payer in outbound transport, mainly following the disbandment of its commercial fleet out of group and personal interests. Starting with 1995, the position of net foreign payer has been present in tourism as well.

The interests Romania has to pay for its external debts add to the deficit existing in the balance of goods and services. However, sometimes the deficit in the foreign current account is a little lower than the trade deficit because of some funds transfers to Romania (representing non-redeemable assistance, such as PHARE funds, nongovernmental contributions, aids for foundations, and mainly repatriation of the money earned by Romanians abroad).

In any case, the evolution of the current account deficit strictly follows that of the trade deficit because of the overwhelming weight of the latter. How is the current account deficit financed? The figures are indicative.

The fundamental proportion – more than 4/5 – in financing belongs to the long-term foreign credits and to foreign direct investments. In the first post-December years, credits were predominant and investments negligible. The reason is well known: delay in starting reforms discouraged the foreign investors and the credits granted to Romania were mainly from the international financial institutions. In the meantime, the situation has changed a little. During 1994–2000, the direct investments contributed 50% and exceeded the long-term foreign credits.

The so-called portfolio investments – on the capital market – had a weak contribution to financing.

Therefore, during 1991–2000, the long-term credits and also direct and portfolio investments covered integrally the deficit in the foreign current account; to the end of that interval they even permitted reimbursement of the credits contracted from IMF at the beginning of the interval. In such a situation how did the National Bank succeed to collect more than $2.5 billion in the same interval and how was the Romanian banking system able to have net deposits of $ 920 billion in foreign banks? In both cases, the evolutions were significant in relation to what we know to have happened in economy.

The National Bank strove to gather hard currency from the domestic market or directly from abroad. However, the economic situation and the foreign payments were not encouraging. Out of political and economic-financial reasons, the Bank was even obliged to consume from its reserves, despite their precarious level. Likewise, the banking system constantly tried to make safety deposits in foreign banks: their interests would have relaxed the tensions in the system. Similarly to the case of National Bank, those deposits had to be consumed in the same years for the same reasons. However, both the National Bank and the banking system succeeded in gathering some net money.

The figures show that the source could have been neither direct and portfolio investments nor long-term foreign credits: the entries in all these cases were hardly able to cover the deficit in the foreign current account, generated mainly by exports being massively exceeded by imports.

Curious and unlikely as it might seem, Romania's balance of payments (calculated according to IMF recommendations) calls this source "Errors and omissions". The assets must always equal liabilities and a deficit or surplus on the balance of payments refers to an imbalance. The differences are included under "Errors and omissions". Obviously if a deficit exists in the current account, if the net entries – foreign credits, direct and portfolio foreign investments – cover the respective deficit only, and, despite this, the National Bank and the banking system still have currency reserves or deposits, money must have come from somewhere else. It is real, good money, I have to insist, that has been inserted under "Errors and omissions"

"Errors and omissions" had constantly the sign "+" and contributed to financing or covering the deficit in the current foreign account. The contribution was always rather important: one third during 1991–2000 and almost one third in 1997–2000. In absolute figures, the contribution was more than $4.2 billion between 1991 and 2000.

There is no doubt that there are trans-frontier financial transfers within black economy. It seems that black economy transfers money abroad. It certainly does. This money may appear in other countries' balances of payments. At the same time, black economy introduces money in Romania by: illegal transportations, transit taxes for drugs, arms, cigarettes, alcoholic drinks, and other contraband goods, commissions for laundering money in Romanian casinos, etc. We do not know exactly the amount of money leaked to other countries and consequently the amount of the financial transfers in the black economy. However, it is certain that "Errors and omissions" in the Romanian official balance include mainly the entries from black economy. But for these entries the financing situation of the current account would have been tenser.

The state of things in 1999 was relevant. In that year, Romania, on the verge of becoming defaulted on payment, had no access to other foreign money than that got from exports and had to limit its expenditures. The IMF program to reduce domestic demand and to block Romania's access to foreign resources operated efficiently: Romania was forced to reduce by $1.6 billion the net consumption of foreign resources and, inland, to reduce the average income by about 4 wages of the 12 monthly wages. However, the decrease in the standard of living was milder than these adjustments because "Errors and omissions" financed more than 60% (!) of the deficit. That was the contribution of black economy!

The more numerous western studies incriminating the countries in transition because they do not stop black economy seem rather hypocritical at least in the case of Romania: in 1999 when Romania received no resource support from abroad and it was asked to reduce its external debts (despite the social explosion menacing it), it was black economy that saved it from economic and social collapse. It was not an honorable thing at all but that is it!

However, Romania cannot rely on entries in "Errors and omission" for further financing the foreign deficit: it cannot control them. It should rely on net entries as foreign credits and investments. The prospects for the future financing of important deficits are very unlikely although, according to the present international standards, the sums are ridiculous. Unfortunately, Romania has already sold what was profitable (and it made bad deals only) and what is still to be sold will be even less profitable.

It cannot expect investments from green-field projects both because of the corruption and of the lower and lower general interest in the area.

Therefore, foreign credits are the only solution left. It is however unrealistic and unprofitable to rely on them only.

38.2. - 1999 Explosion

In 1999, the tragedy existing in the current account and in the financial and capital accounts exploded. On the one hand, the increasing current account deficits after 1994 accumulated an important external debt; on the other hand, imprudent and nonprofessional financing of these deficits led to an outrageous payments rescheduling. Because of the massive three-year loans contracted in 1996 by the National Bank, at political command, the external debt generated in 1999 a service of about $3 billion for a less debt than $9 billion: an absurd situation that proved Bank's lack of responsibility in managing the external debt.

The problems generated in 1999 by the foreign payments influenced the future economic policy, Romania's relation with IMF, and the western attitude towards Romania.

From the viewpoint of foreign payments, Romania concluded 1999 with an unusual balance: external debt decreased with 10% in one year only. Actually, such a thing had not happened since Ceausescu: the dictator's ego determined gradual reduction to final liquidation of the external debt by stopping foreign credits and paying installments and interests in advance with the result that Romania became economically drained and started to lag behind. The after-effects have remained.

In 1999, the reduction of the external debt was determined by the recipes IMF prescribed for Romania. The simple formula was to close Romania's access to international capital markets by refusing to give it the certificate it deserved. By decreasing the external debt in this way, the credit was no longer a development instrument.

The dimension of reducing the external debt was not usual either. It meant an amputation of the net consumption in foreign resources, about 3% of GDP, which was too much for Romania, then in serious economic drop. The two factors, decrease of external debt and reduction of GDP, meant a dramatic adjustment strongly felt in the population's living standard. It is a wonder that Romania did not explode socially. In fact, part of the foreign adjustment was supported by the currency reserve of the National Bank and some other part was transferred to the account of the domestic public debt.

38.3. What has IMF actually aimed at?

The 1999 balance strongly posed the problem of the sense of Romania's relation with IMF. It is agreed with good reasons indeed that Romania cannot live far from the world financial community and IMF is one of the latter's pillars; we like it or not the relation with IMF is better than the absence of such a relation because it offers credibility abroad. However, such an argument is both insufficient and proves the lack of genuine arguments. The agreement Romania tried in vain to conclude with IMF in 1999 was concluded only when it became practically useless because the debt peak for the foreign payments had already passed. However, following this agreement the international agencies did neither change the rating for Romania nor did the country attract foreign investments. Quite the contrary: it cancelled fiscal facilities and thus sent away the few foreign investors existing in Romania.

More than that: in the most difficult period for Romania, IMF sent it on the international market of private capital and forced it to borrow or, otherwise, it would not receive the credibility certificate. Practically, IMF invited private capital to fleece it and some other poor countries (Ecuador, Pakistan, Ukraine, etc.). Luckily, such an absolutely incorrect experiment was rejected by the American private capital that refused to lend.

According to IMF, Romania had to borrow from the private foreign market following a somewhat "moral" criterion: the so-called burden sharing. IMF asked the international private capital to shoulder the responsibility and take part in saving the countries in a slump. However, as IMF could not make private capital accept such a part, it did no longer allow the borrowing countries to pay their external debts to private sources from foreign funds got from public sources (IMF, World, Bank, European Union, etc.).

As expected, the private capital market refused "to share" any burden with IMF and the respective countries got the message: they can rely on nobody but on themselves.

Unfortunately, the above experiment shows that there are IMF has-beens who have made fetishes of their own creations, and now, faced with fabulous failures in numerous countries, are seized with authority crises and intransigencies.

The dramatic situation in 1999 seems to have been more complex in Romania. In 1999, when the maturity date had come, the Romanian officials were simply bombarded by the United States and Western Europe advising or demanding them to start procedures for postponing foreign payments. Concretely, they wanted to rollover or to delay the payments of the securities the National Bank had issued in 1996 on the international private capital market and to reschedule other components of the external debt.

Apparently a good advice: the loans due for payment in the near future would have been converted into others, repayable until some more distant date. Such rescheduling would have allowed Romania to relax a little. However, there was another side of the issue that aroused suspicion.

First, the demand for postponing the due date is an implicit recognition of payment default but also a negative signal for creditors and for the possible investors in that country.

Second, the postponement is not free of charge but involves penalties and new interests.

Third, in the concrete situation of Romania's external debt in 1999, postponing payments would have been a contrived, almost comical action. Romania's external debt had two important components: the main one was the so-called constitutional one (money borrowed from international financial institutions such as IMF, World Bank, EBRD, or from other international organizations, e.g. European Union); the latter component was represented by the securities issued first (in 1996) by the National Bank and then (in 1997) by the Romanian government on the international markets following Romania's re-entering these markets after 15 years of interdiction.

As far as the former component is concerned, Romania had already paid its debts to the European Union and was ready to reimburse to IMF. The installments and credits got from the World Bank and EBRD were still to be paid but they were not due for payment yet. Therefore, Romania had nothing to re-schedule in this component.

The rollovers were the latter component. The first securities issued by the National Bank three years before were due for payment at the agreed interest. The National Bank was advised to ask the foreigners holding Romanian securities to accept the delay of the dates at which they were redeemable; following negotiations the payments would have been postponed and the new interests calculated according to Romania's rating.

The story of those securities, redeemable in 1999, is rather interesting. They were issued by the National Bank when there was not any agreement between Romania and IMF; the latter stopped financing when the Romanian party had defaulted on its loans. However, how could Romania get such an advantageous financing despite the fact that IMF had stopped it? Perhaps the future will enlighten us!

CHAPTER 39

Is the Monetary Council a solution for Romania?

There were serious suspicions that more or less hidden interests wanted Romania to default on the payment. The international rating agency Standard & Poor's announced the investors that Romania together with Ivory Coast and Zimbabwe were at risk of defaulting on the payments in that very year. *The Economist* even included Romania among the list of the countries that had negotiated the securities issued by them, namely they had postponed the redeeming of those securities. It is useless to remind that Romania had done nothing of the kind; on the contrary, it had tried to oppose to the numerous recommendations asking it to renegotiate the securities.

It was therefore likely that the respective "errors" were on purpose and reflected some opinions in the international financial community according to which the Monetary Council would be a better solution for Romania than a normal regime with central bank, monetary policy, and currency exchange policy. However, the reason might have been the opinion that Romania had been unable to solve its problems related to inflation and a stable currency.

A Monetary Council regime means that the national currency is strictly related to a certain hard currency and supposes the abandonment of the monetary policy and of the institution that governs it, i.e. the central bank (National Bank in the case of Romania).

In a Monetary Council regime the national currency becomes the reference hard currency (euro or dollar). As a principle, the country inflation aligns itself with inflationist depreciation of the reference currency and it can be 1–3% yearly, as in the USA or in the zero zones. However the consequences are terrible. If imports do not tally with export profits, the amount of national currency has to be automatically reduced, together with social expenses and with wages. The budget can no longer borrow money from the national currency issuer; it has to limit the expenses as a function of the real incomes and of its ability to borrow real money on the market. Those opposing to the Monetary Council regime emphasize this very fact: the system can only operate in an economy that observes the fiscal and budgetary discipline. In a country like Romania where taxes and duties are not paid, such a regime would simply block the budget and social security and finally the whole economy. Although the Monetary Council's role is to eliminate non-performing activities, it cannot change real economy.

However, a country should have a certain currency reserve when entering a Monetary Council regime. If not, that reserve could be borrowed from abroad. Bulgaria entered a Monetary Council regime with the equivalent of about $3 billion. Taking into account that the net average wage in Romania is hardly around $100 monthly, we should need at least $10 billion. Therefore, before being forced to adopt a Monetary Council regime, Romania should be first pushed to reduce the net average wage to $ 25–30 monthly as happened in Bulgaria. Such a thing could only happen after economic or financial collapse as Bulgaria experienced. Therefore, adoption of a Monetary Council regime cannot be a prophylactic action.

CHAPTER 40

"Externalization" vs. "internalization" of economic problems

Isarescu became prime minister after the terrible year 1999, so there was not much choice for him. In fact he continued the policy of Isarescu, the ex-governor of the National Bank, to internalize the serious problems of the Romanian economy, i.e. took them out of the sphere of the external payments and transferred them to the domestic budget. Following such a policy, the ex-governor Isarescu and the then the Prime Minister Radu Vasile had avoided the default on the external payments on the expense of the state budget that had almost compromised its basic functions.

Isarescu government had to continue the "internalization" policy of the economic problems since practically it had no access to foreign resources. The same thing had happened during Vasile government with the only difference that now economy offered businesses a second wind (by reducing profit taxation). In exchange, the population was even more heavily taxed by an increased VAT for products and services. However, as the elections were close, Isarescu had to avoid a possible explosion and to finance somehow the existing social parameters.

Financing was partly achieved by topping the budgetary deficit agreed with IMF. Another part came from the inauspicious stretching of resources by reviving the "traditional" exports. However, the most important part was financed by inflation. The attempt to keep the level of exports implied severe devaluation of the *leu* and it was the population that finally footed the bill: on the one hand the prices of the imported products increased and on the other hand, the monopolistic companies kept increasing prices despite decrease in demand.

40.1. Nastase "reversal"

Nastase government started at the end of 2000 in more favorable circumstances created by the economic refloating during Isarescu government. They followed a quite different strategy.

For long years Romania had tried to stand more or less on its two feet. Nastase government aimed at relaxing the problems of domestic economy at the expense of increasing external debt. If foreign loans had been convenient the attempt would have not to be incriminated but the external money was very expensive. However, the attempt proved to be dangerous if foreign credits were used, directly or not, to support social security and to save the workplaces for unprofitable activities more often than not without a market.

The origin of that attempt to reverse the content of economic policy could be found in "The White Book of Assumption of Government in December 2002". The book compares the situation in 1996 with that in 2000 using the so-called "pentagon of performances" (economic development, inflation, unemployment, budgetary deficit in GDP, and current account deficit in GDP equivalent). Based on statistical data, the White Book emphasizes the same annual inflation rate and about the same budgetary deficit in GDP equivalent. The other three indices were different: double economic development and about half unemployment in 1996; the foreign current account deficit in GDP equivalent had been almost double in 1996, namely the net consumption of foreign resources had been two times higher. However, the lower net consumption of foreign resources in 2000 entailed feeble economic activity and severer unemployment.

Nastase government assumed the conclusion and tried to rapidly increase the appeal for foreign financing. The White Book does invite to such a policy trying to peddle the idea that "Romania is under-indebted abroad". There is no doubt that Romania having a public external debt of only $300/inhabitant is under-indebted in comparison with Hungary ($1560/inhabitant), Czech Republic ($1250/inhabitant), or Bulgaria ($870/inhabitant). However you can only borrow if you find someone to lend you money. The cost of that money is equally important. If it is too high you can finally become defaulted on payment. Bulgaria was in such a situation because its creditors refused to lend it about several hundreds million dollars! It is true that the creditors might become more benevolent after having punished you. However, a penance is a penance and it is very expensive.

Comparisons with Hungary, Poland, or Czech Republic are not correct either. In these countries the debts are paid from investments that do not create vicious circles. Nastase government can try to experiment the system of high indebtedness but the reimbursement can become an explosive problem: Romania is in a difficult situation and the foreign money can only be found at very high costs.

From the beginning of 2001, Nastase government assumed foreign commitments of more than 2.5% GDP equivalent: credits from international financial institutions, loans with governmental warranties, and mainly €600 million-valued public securities issued on the international market of the private capital.

The loan was presented as a success of Nastase government. According to the Romanian standards the sum was very important: the market reacted favorably and the subscription result came shortly after the famous international rating agency Standard & Poor's had improved practically all the risk marks for Romania from B- to B and from C to B, respectively. The pressure of the external payments ceased, economy started to develop a little, Romania's currency reserve increased significantly, and exports seemed to invigorate. However, I question the promptness of Standard & Poor's: in 1999 the agency announced that Romania would be at risk of defaulting on payments although that was not the case; in 2000, it did not only refuse to improve the qualifiers but also warned that Romania would never get money from the international market of the private capital if the then opposition would ascend to power. The then opposition, PSDR, ascended to power and paradoxically, the agency became quite indulgent.

Had they become friendlier? We can only be glad to have won their favor.

However, the high level of the risk increase above the basic interest explains the interest in Romanian securities and in issue oversubscription. Of all the securities admitted on the international market, the Romanian ones had almost the highest interest. For the buyers of the Romanian securities the profits were among the highest possible on the market. Obviously, the cost Romania paid was among the highest as well.

The thing is that if the amounts Romania got could be invested entirely, and not used for consumption as well, there is none domestic placement profitable enough to cover such costs and to ensure reimbursement. However, Nastase government did not seem to be concerned about that issue and thought more about what was going to happen in 2002. The PSDR Cabinet needed money on a short term because they wanted to prevent people's dissatisfaction with the government before 2002 when NATO was expected to extend again to the East. Had the answer been affirmative for Romania, the Romanian officials hoped that NATO would not allow one of its member countries in difficulty. Had the answer been "no" again it might not have been so important what happened with the external debt.

IMF toned down the enthusiasm of Nastase government concerning external indebtedness. In order to get the stand-by agreement, IMF asked, among others, the reducing of the appeal for external indebtedness, both directly by limiting the foreign credits ceiling and indirectly by reducing to 5% GDP equivalent the current account deficit in 2002.

40.2. Not credits, but investments!

On a long term Romania should be less enthusiastic about external debts that will generate payment difficulties because of the high costs. The country should better concentrate on attracting foreign direct investments that do not create such problems.

From that point of view, the law for stimulating significant direct investments, passed by Nastase government in the first half of 2001, seems to be better than the €600 million loan despite IMF and World Bank opposition.

The ideal solution for Romania is to attract direct foreign investments. Whereas foreign credits are very expensive and the investments on the capital market are volatile, namely unstable, direct investments mean direct involvement in business, technology and management transfer – a capital that does not create external debt. Direct investments can make Romanian economy efficient, irrespective of the obstacles raised by the state sector, by trade unions, or by parties.

IMF and the World Bank drew the attention that the facilities created by such a law could generate a "market distortion" and were against it. However it is absurd to ask a poor country like Romania to be more liberalistic than wealthier countries since similar facilities exist in those countries. It is even more absurd to think that a country like Romania could destabilize the international market relations.

As Prime Minister Nastase rightly emphasized, the countries in the Central Europe have stimulating regulations in this field. The products made by attracting foreign investments in this way are successfully sold in Romania as well by using the customs facilities mutually agreed between the respective countries and Romania within CEFTA. Likewise, IMF insisted on a possible decrease of the budgetary collection following those facilities. Of course, the issue should not be ignored but it is not very important either since on a short term the activity volume will increase as a result of foreign investments.

However, a major problem is the discretionary enforcement of the law in Romania: any law in Romania should be carefully worded to avoid misinterpretation and quite precise not to allow officials' or politicians' interferences. Exemption from customs duties for investment goods is not substantiated enough: the law practically encourages imports from the USA and from the Asian countries; the imports from the European Union and those from CEFTA – which represent the majority – are tax exempted. Therefore, the Romanian-made products are at a disadvantage.

In its present wording and within the given context the law does not represent what it wanted to be: a general and final regulation for direct investments and a background element of a stable business environment.

40.3. The ping-pong of facilities

In the absence of a clear conception and similarly clear game rules, generally assumed by the state authority, by the parliamentary political parties, and by the businesspeople the wording of such a law was subject to the same contradictory pressures as before: budgetary constraints; pressure from the domestic capital; the opposed pressure for attracting foreign capital. The result was a kind of mish-mash hardly to be enforced. The situation during the RDC-DP administration repeated almost identically.

The legislation left by the Vacaroiu government reflected a clear conception: linear facilities for investors, some additional facilities for small businesses, and a series of facilities for major investments (the so-called "Daewoo law"). Although the law rewarded the seriously involved investors it became the butt of both the domestic capital (that considered it discriminating) and of the western investors (because it repaid a South-Korean company). The RDC-PD administration revoked the law and passed an emergency ordinance, fiscally difficult to enforce, that provided gradual facilities as a function of the investment value.

In those conditions, at the end of 1997 an emergency ordinance was passed according to which the Romanian capital and the foreign one were subject to the same conditions. The ordinance was clear, linear and simple: facilities were given for setting up the social capital only. Norms were established for the economic operation concerning the crucial problem of calculating the base for profit taxation. The bill was passed in the Chamber of Deputies with the agreement of PSDR then in opposition.

The things were not so smooth in the Chamber of Senators. Those who at a particular juncture had demagogically asked equal treatment used the parliamentary debate to introduce all kind of amendments for transferring public money into their own pockets. Viorel Catarama who pretended to be a liberal had the most baleful influence. Thus the ordinance changed into something quite different and it finally became a law. The then president Emil Constantinescu promulgated it although everybody knew that with no budgetary support the law cannot be applied. Two months later IMF took a tough stand and the law was abrogated for the 1999 tax year (and then for 2000). In this way the norms for economic operation included in the initial ordinance were abrogated as well and the situation became disastrous. In the absence of any unitary regulations in the field and under the budgetary pressure, Vasile government adopted an emergency ordinance that empowered the government to grant special facilities to major investors (the so-called "Renault law" that granted important facilities for the French concern that took over Dacia factory). A dangerous precedent was thus set! IMF was furious: it could not accept facilities for the major investors after having rejected those for the minor ones. On the other hand, the important investors accepted the Renault facilities as a basis of discussion only. Therefore, Isareascu government had to grant Renault-type facilities to the German investors from Continental and to the American ones from Solectron. After that, IMF abrogated the ordinance.

Under those conditions, Nastase government assumed office. Practically, there was no regulation in the field – an advantage for solving the problem. Unfortunately, the government put the wrong leg foremost and offered facilities, as a positive discrimination, for small and middle organizations without correlating them with the general regulations. These organizations took immediate advantage of the customs reductions and imported a lot, mainly as intermediaries. The imports exploded and the trade deficit reached again incendiary quotas posing the same old financing problems. More than that, the budget was simply suffocated. The law practically repeated the 1997 ordinance: the only difference was that the same provisions operated only for the economic organizations that invested more than $ 1 million.

If the law wanted to attract important foreign investors the effect might be disappointing. Fiscal facilities, mainly those for profit taxation, have a marginal role for the large international companies which calculate their profit at the general level of their production and trade network. They use the "transfer prices" among the components of this network so that the profits appear in countries where taxation level is low (more often than not in tax havens). These companies direct their investments to one place or another as a function of: political stability, size of the market, corruption level, etc. If the place is the Balkan area, if the legislation changes but bureaucracy and corruption remain, if the people are not very industrious, and the cost of social security per workplace is high then the full-scale foreign capitals look for opportunities in other places of the world.

40.4. Direct foreign investments – need for a "critical mass"

Structural changes can only take place in Romania if the direct foreign investments reach $10–12 billion, i.e. about $5–6 billion more than at present. At such a critical mass the foreign direct investments would become a kind of engine that could push or pull the rest of economy, no matter if the politicians or institutions wanted it or no.

In Romania, the direct foreign investments, beyond the above-mentioned critical mass, would solve at least the following problems: surmount institutional incapacity, stop the resource waste in non-performing activities, indirectly reduce the pork-barrel politics, and mainly promote the construction component of the reform.

For a while, the direct foreign investments in Romania are at risk if they use the Romanian market only. They simply cannot avoid the tyranny of the small figures in Romanian economy. They have to take into account that the average wage in Romania is about $100 and the Romanians' purchasing power is very low. Likewise, the repatriation of important profits might be difficult taking into account the currency restrictions determined by the limited export returns. An export-oriented production of the direct foreign investments could gradually, but quite rapidly eliminate restrictions.

Of course all these are simple hypotheses. The important direct foreign investments will not come to Romania as long as the Balkans have not become a stable area and this thing might never happen; as long as the business environment in Romania remains unfriendly; as long as bureaucracy and corruption flourish; as long as the problem of real-estate property has not been solved; as long as the trade unions have not accepted restructuring, etc.

Without a critical mass in the foreign investments Romania will not be able to develop. If unfortunately it is obliged to develop without foreign investments nobody knows how far in the future such a thing is possible.

CHAPTER 41

Romania – West: 2nd run-off

The prospects of the Romanian economy are conditioned by the future position of the western countries towards Romania. The year 2000 opened a new page in the post-communist history of the relations between Romania and the West and things must be made clear once for ever. The result of the 2000 elections can be used as an argument both for Romania's exclusion and for its support. However, from both points of view the necessary clarifications can no longer be postponed after the long ambiguity that used to govern Romania's relation with the West in the 1st run-off (the decade that passed from the events in December 1989).

For more than a decade the Romanian political class had done almost nothing essential for Romania to join the western world: the ownership problem had not been solved; none of the basic rules of a market economy had been observed.

On the other hand, the westerners' intentions were not clear either: no major involvement in Romania, no money, no influence. From the West, Romania hardly got money to keep it alive. No western power structure, in sight or secret, was genuinely interested in Romania. Russia, in exchange, insistently and unequivocally tried to keep Romania within its sphere of influence. The Russian Secret Services present in Romania had almost no Romanian or foreign counterweight. The western attitude towards Romania was indifference. In the first seven years of transition they pretended that their lack of interest had political reasons since Romania had a communist leadership. In fact, Iliescu's regime was the ideal alibi for the hand-off western policy towards Romania. In the following four years, economic reasons were invoked. Because of economic reasons Romania was not eligible for NATO. The same economic precariousness discouraged western investments in Romania. All pro-West signals of Constantinescu's administration were ignored. Strangely enough that administration received less western money than the previous one. In these conditions the economic failure deepened and their pro-western attitude turned against them in the 2000 elections.

However, paroxysm was reached in 1999. While Romania was praised for its pro-NATO attitude – an absurd position, more pro-NATO than the NATO-member countries – the same Romania was economically pushed to bankruptcy. In 1999 Romania had to pay an important part of its external debts. As it received no support it had to pay back more than it had received from the West. It is a miracle that it could avoid collapse.

The year 1999 ended atypically: the European Union took the historic decision of inviting Romania to take part to integrating negotiations. Politically, there was no alternative. What happened in 2000 was typical of the situation preceding the Helsinki decision. The Romanian political class did nothing concrete to honor that decision and the European Union chose to wait for the general elections at the end of 2000.

Neither the governing political class nor PSDR in opposition – and probably nobody in the West – had anticipated the results of November 26, 2000 vote. The situation in Romania – better characterized by the formula *too much theft, too much poverty* – had been ignored. Anyhow, if the political class was responsible for *too much theft* there is no doubt that the West had its major contribution to the *too much poverty* part.

Of course, the West has no obligation to Romania and if they have no interest here Romania has nothing to expect from the West. But this issue needs clarifications and the western intentions were not clear at all.

The international situation might speed up the necessary clarifications. Up to now the only certitude is that Romania has been included in the first wave of the western expansion eastward. We do not know if Romania will be included in the second wave but things might follow the same "scenario" as before.

A major test for the western intentions towards Romania was the visa issue. The abolition of the visa requirements for Romanians, starting with 2002, does not only mean the end of a humiliating discrimination, but also a change of Romania's statute in Europe. At the beginning of the 1990s the delimitations in the visa requirements prefigured the new borders of the NATO and of the European Union. The delimitations are now economic and as they grow netter and stronger the handicap of those left aside grows as well. However, Romania is admitted to be in someday.

More than a decade has passed since the demolition of the communist-built wall through Berlin. New walls are being built today in Europe and they are more impenetrable because they divide economic worlds. The former disparities between East and West have become deeper and more complex now.

There is an important gap between Central and Western Europe but it is going to be bridged in time. There is also an already severe disparity between Central and Eastern Europe and it seems to deepen.

Romania represents a notorious economic failure, the result of the stalling policy of the Bucharest governments in implementing economic reforms. Unfortunately, Romania is not the only economic failure in the ex-communist area: the failures are common here and the little success is an exception.

Of course, there was no historical precedent and no experience in passing from command economy to market economy. Therefore, lack of success should wonder no one. In fact, the West was the winner in the Cold War but it was not prepared for the collapse of communism: it had no strategy to help the ex-communist countries bear the ineluctable shocks caused by the economic-social changes and, after that, to help them follow the new way.

Some success has however been recorded in such Central-European countries as Czech Republic, Poland, or Hungary. (The examples of Baltic Countries and Slovenia are not relevant: due to their small sizes, injections of several billions were enough to significantly and rapidly change their states). Besides their better inheritance and the determination of their political class, the success of the three countries is due to their strong western partners that made serious investments there and waived their debts.

There is no doubt they deserved help but the decisions were political, not economic. Their armies – ex-members of Warsaw Treaty – were considered compatible with the NATO standards because it was politically decided to be so. Their secret services that had not been more humane than those in other ex-communist countries were fit to join the western secret services because it was politically right. The influx of foreign capital to those countries had political reasons as well

The rest of countries in the area had all the reasons to score failures: lack of institutional capacity, wrong management, corruption, etc. Obviously, the West cannot be made responsible for their failure and has no obligation to support them economically. However, the only conclusion to be drawn is that failure could be avoided only in the countries where the West decided to commit itself to large-scale financial support.

CHAPTER 42

September 11 and the NATO extension

The second major test for the western intentions towards Romania was the decision taken in the autumn of 2002 concerning the NATO extension eastward.

NATO is a political and military organization, not an economic one although it makes of economic performances the almost single criterion for closing the so-called "open doors" in front of the politically undesirable countries. Greece and Turkey had no economic performance but they joined NATO out of strategic reasons exclusively. Poland and Hungary joined NATO under communist administrations whereas Romania was not admitted although its leaders had long been imprisoned by communists. If we accept that Romania had no real chance of being admitted to NATO in 1997, the situation is identical in 2002. However, if we accept the idea that it had a chance then, in 2002 the chances are worse. Its economy has kept degrading for three years and it has been in the latest two years that it has started to revive. Politically, the situation is not encouraging at all: the PSDR administration has done nothing to cultivate the western governments.

The political decision in 2002 will consider the new situation in the Eastern and South-Eastern Europe. Milosevic's democratic overthrow has not solved the problems automatically. The conflict centre has moved to Macedonia, following a scenario almost similar to that in Kosovo, with the only difference that NATO does no longer support a new Albanese autonomy movement. Following the elections in Moldova and Kiev going over to the same boat with Moscow, Russia has practically reached Romania's border. The position of the Kishinev administration will force Bucharest to ask the West clarify the issue of its western border: that will be either

Romania's eastern border or Romania will remain in the grey zone. Such a decision does not depend on Romania but on strategic and political interests transcending it. The NATO extension might be part of a possible new agreement between Russia and the United States. President Bush may warn Russia that NATO will stretch from the Baltic Sea to the Black Sea but Washington may choose one or other candidate according to the global interest transcending the area.

However, the world equation, and mainly the Russian–American one – that interests Romania – has became more complex after the terrorist attacks of September 11, 2001.

The officials in Bucharest adopted the right position against terrorism: an unambiguous choice between life and death. Romania's airspace and terrestrial space was put at the USA and NATO's disposal in case they would have needed them. Romania was on the American side not necessarily because it wanted to join NATO but because it could only be against terrorism.

If Romania will join or not NATO in the second wave of its extension is still to be seen. However, it is certain that the relations between Romania and the West will finally leave the grey zone.

President Iliescu say that there is no tragedy if Romania does not join NATO in 2002. He is perfectly right. In fact Romania experiences another tragedy: an economic tragedy against a background of geopolitical one! It does not need the NATO umbrella to get itself protected by some enemy: it hopes that under that umbrella some investors will "invade" it.

CHAPTER 43

Integration into the European Union: a pure political decision!

The third test of the western intentions towards Romania will be a possible integration, some day in the future, of the country into the European Union. Of course the chances will be greater if Romania has been first admitted to NATO.

43.1. Lagging behind other candidate-countries

For the time being Romania is the last among the other candidate-countries that want to join European Union. Ten long years have passed since the integration option was declared and Romania has done nothing to prepare itself for this integration. Not even when an association agreement became effective and the frail Romanian economy in a regime of gradual customs disarmament had to face the competitive western European economies. It is common knowledge that the basic preparation for integration is an economic one and not just paperwork. However, Romania is as badly prepared for integration as it was when it expressed its option. Under the pressure of an unproductive and loss-generating sector, Romanian economy will be an eternal loser in the international competition that keeps increasing.

All those governing after December 1989 should shoulder the responsibility for this situation. Petre Roman government started the reform but it started it disastrously with cheap populism and with half measures and mess-ups in the real-estate issue that blocked privatization and were not clarified. The Iliescu administrations as a whole, and mainly Vacaroiu government, are responsible for the dangerous reform delays, and for disequilibria in the domestic and foreign accounts of the State. The RDC–DP administration was responsible for not initiating genuine economic reforms either.

The responsibility belongs to all the post-December governs because the integrating preparation is a long process that should have started more than ten years ago and has not started yet. Did Romania appraise the advantages it could have relied on and did it try to conserve or to improve them should negotiation talks for a possible integration have started? Did Romania do anything to get rid of the unproductive economic sector that could sideline it? Did it take any economic measure able to face the predictable consequences of the gradual reduction of the protection level by customs? The European Union is economically so far that Romania cannot practically reach the lowest standards required.

Romania's presence in the European Union structures would dilute the latter, or might even hammer it.

However, at the Helsinki summit, the European Union decided to invite Romania to integration negotiations. Politically, the West could not have left Romania and Bulgaria aside (the only "problem-countries" among those wanting to integrate) because it would have implicitly recognized what it rejects officially: a new division of Europe.

Economically, Romania was not at all eligible for integration negotiations. However, that was the first concrete signal. If the European Union decided to move its eastern border to Romania's eastern border it means that Romania can escape its "eastern condemnation" that meant not only economic poverty but also a state of mind, of implacable victim, and hopeless loser.

Unfortunately, the message the Romanian political class transmitted abroad was a rather equivocal one. Romania's attitude would not be that important if the Helsinki decision to integrate it were firm and final. What if the

Helsinki decision was just a test or rather a compromise between those who accepted Romania's integration and those who did not agree with it?

It is not the moment to indulge ourselves in illusions and to consider that Romania's fate has been decided and that it will adhere willy-nilly. If the European Union position adopted in Helsinki is strategic, but not irreversible, then their good will remains purely platonic until Romania has honored it properly. Platonic meaning that they will give no money. Without money Romania cannot stop falling down even if its political class finally decides to wake up.

Before Helsinki Romania was in a vicious circle with no prospects at all. The decision in Helsinki seems to have broken that circle and opened the way for little hope. However, what happened in Romania following Helsinki was not encouraging at all for the westerners who supported Romania's cause.

The abolition of the visa requirements for Romanians was a blank check the European Union gave to the Nastase government that had to prove that it was able to commit itself to the demands of the organization.

It is true that after the tragedy of September 11, 2001 the European West realized that the Orthodox, poor as they were, were Christians and therefore closer to them than the fanatic Islamists wearing bombs in their belts.

We do not know yet if Romania will or will not be a member of the European Union. That depends not only on Romania's economic progress but also on the political goodwill of the Western-European decision makers.

43.2. The rent belongs to the European Union

Following the association agreement with the European Union, Romania has practically got a foot in door. Starting with 1995 a free-exchange zone has been created for industrial products by gradual reduction to disappearance of the customs duties for the mutual flow of goods.

Within the free zone, the small and unproductive Romanian industry has to face directly, with no protection at all a strong and competitive industry and the Romanian products will meet the exacting standards of the European Union market.

However, the diagnosis of the Brussels Commission on the integration stage is unequivocal: on a long term Romania is not able to face the competition pressures and the market forces within the European Union.

It is true: Romania is not able to face either competition pressures or market forces within the European Union. Still, Romania is forced to face those pressures because, by achieving the provisions in the free exchange zone, it is already within the trade space regulated by the European Union. An export from France, for instance, meets the same conditions – no customs obstacles – no matter if it is sent to Germany or to Romania. Customs protection has disappeared. It is only for competitiveness to decide.

How can Romania handle such a situation although it is not able to? With a huge price indeed! It is systematically wasting its economic substance. The competitive imports from the European Union are financed with exports from either cheap workforce *(lohn)* or raw materials (wood, timber, scrap metals, aluminum, etc.), both of them stretched almost to their limits.

Maybe another calendar of the customs disarmaments should have been adopted. Maybe the Romanian negotiators in 1993–1994 did not realize the long haul to competitiveness of the mediocre Romanian industry or maybe they were too optimistic. In any case, Romania has to start from the actual state of things and get by. Even if it is not able to, Romania has to face directly the competitive pressures within the European Union.

The European Union might regret their decision to invite Romania to integration negotiations. However, no matter how small and unimportant the Romanian market is, it is profitable because in a free-exchange zone the competitiveness advantage belongs to the Western-European products.

In the case of Romania, the difference in competitiveness is also reflected by the one million-dollar trade deficit in its relations with the European Union. In 2000 the deficit was about $800 million. In exchange, the unredeemable assistance Romania got from the European Union was of about $600 million and started being paid in 2001. Therefore, the European Union extracts, by the competitiveness differential that belongs to it, the differential advantage rent before suffering the consequences generated by enforcing, together with the candidate-countries, the other two main principles: free circulation of capitals and free circulation of persons.

Obviously, the last two principles are correlative. Frankly, nobody can say exactly which of the two sides is lest prepared to enforce those principles: the European Union or the candidate-countries. Let us speak about Romania only. The enforcement of the principle of the capital free circulation may ruin a country like Romania. However there is not much difference from the present situation when the trans-frontier protection is practically absent and Romania cannot prevent the capital being taken abroad. In exchange, the European Union is suspicious about the enforcement of the principle of persons' free circulation.

The European Union would keep the present state of things if they were able to: with the rent got from enforcing the principle of goods free circulation and without the disadvantage entailed by enforcing the principle of persons' free circulation. However, they cannot do that and will have to admit at least part of the candidate-countries.

Following the tragic event of September 11, 2001, the European Union will have no reason at all to give up either the economic and political coagulation it has devised among the present member-countries or the extension towards the Central European countries. However, the amplitude and rhythm of the extension eastward will become important reflection topics. Romania and Bulgaria will be at a disadvantage both if the extension is considered from the viewpoints of the "dilution" risk for the community construction and of the "isolation" from the potentially unstable and explosive Balkan area.

CHAPTER 44

The integration process instead of the absent strategy

Irrespective of the final results, following Romania's invitation to participate to integration negotiation, a new element has raised, with possibly crucial consequences for the Romanian transition.

44.1. There is a way now

Romania left communism but as it had no clear targets it went adrift for years. As the country was getting nowhere the foggy formula "social market economy" seemed to stand for the unhappy hybrid economy developing here.

From the historic Helsinki decision, Romania has got an aim: to join European Union. This seems to be its most important achievement; if it is able or not to meet the required standards seems almost meaningless. Therefore an aim takes shape and the strategy that starts to develop will hopefully discipline efforts and polarize resources to the priority targets.

Under the pressure of the European Union, Romanian political class succeeded somehow to develop a medium-term Strategy – a condition to begin the integration negotiations. The Strategy text included a correct diagnosis of the state of the nation and of the Romanian institutions, and also the main objectives, actions, and measures to be taken.

The correct diagnosis was not an easy task because the political, ideological, and doctrinal approaches were completely different and emphasis could have been placed on one aspect or on the other. However, a kind of consensus has been reached and this is a remarkable thing indeed!

The European Union constraints were very clear. First of all, the text of the Strategy had to be signed by the main political forces, by the social partners, and by the civic society. The mutual declaration issued with that occasion assured that the provisions agreed would be followed and supported irrespective of color of the government in Bucharest.

Brussels imposed another constraint too: the text should emphasize the integration costs, not only its advantages. The Brussels officials clearly expressed their opinion that Romanians were in favor of the integration because they did not know the costs in the first place.

However, Strategy is an optimistic text.

44.2. Will the Strategy change Romania?

There is a question, a big question indeed: how could the Romanian economy and its institutions genuinely change in such a short interval? Will the political class, guilty of the entire economic failure, be able to change? Will the political class be the same in the next five years? Why should they act differently then? Has any measure been adopted to force it to change?

In these conditions how could the parliament and the government become better? They cannot be better than the political class that generates them.

Can the dissolution of authority be stopped? Will the rule of law be finally regarded? Will the necessary laws be adopted and will they be enforced? Will the embezzlement of the public funds be stopped? Will corruption be stopped?

In the absence of a previous or at least concomitant institutional reform there is almost no chance of economic change.

The poor state of the Romanian economy is due to politics. Too much politics and too little economy! Romania can only change when economy has brought politics to its knees.

It is only in two fields – education and health (partly) – that punctual measures are considered. In the other fields the measures are either absent or they are mixed up with all kind of ambiguous formulations. Such words as "there will be followed", "there will be stimulated", "the stimulation will be followed", "measures will be taken for" mean nothing. Unfortunately, the "champion" is the very CHAPTER including structural adjustments in economy that says nothing at all about the way the Government "will stimulate" or "will follow to stimulate".

The Strategy does not appraise the necessary resources for reaching the goals they have in view. One CHAPTER only – the environment one – includes such an appraisal but it belongs to the European Union and represents in fact a hypothetical estimation of Romania's global requirements to meet the minimal environment exigencies of the Union.

Let us see the "restructuring scenario" of the Romanian economy until 2004 that considers "rapid getting through crisis and sound refloating of national economy".

At last several of the premises of this scenario are unrealistic. For instance, it stipulates "increase of saving rate and of domestic accumulation". Because of continuous impoverishment, the rate reached 10–20% GDP equivalent in 1999–2000 and nothing could make it increase much enough in the near future to become a source of investment funds. An inquiry made by the National Institute of Statistics showed that in May-October 2000 the average saving/family was about $0.5.

Several question marks hang over the contribution of the foreign resources relied on. The direct foreign investments should represent 3.9–4.9% GDP yearly. The absolute amounts are not high at the present international standards but they are double or even triple in comparison with the yearly highest entries in the 1990s. In any case, as the resources cannot be controlled, the investment and economic increase scenarios should have at least two variants: with and without contribution of direct foreign investments. Romania must try to stand on its own two feet – as it did in 1999 – with no contribution of foreign resources.

Likewise, the "restructuring scenario" speaks about "reinforcement of financial discipline" but it practically does not provide any measure to stop tax evasion.

The scenario also relies on "a gradual re-monetization of economy in conditions of strictly non-inflationist increase of the monetary base, development of other monetary aggregates by extension and development of the banking instruments, reduction within logical limits of the rate of the minimum reserve requirements, and of the real interest as well". Re-monetization would be a fabulous financing source for national economy but it is a minefield at the same time. A normal economy needs a money supply of 50–60% GDP equivalent to put GDP into action. In Romania, because of poverty and of people's lack of confidence in economy, in national currency, and in public institutions themselves, money change hands very quickly: a money supply of only 20 – 30% GDP equivalent is enough to put GDP into action. Therefore, little money is left on the market to finance real economy. If money in the market exceeds the mentioned limits it rapidly generates inflation. In such conditions, the National Bank both hesitates to issue money and tries to "sterilize" any money "excess". What could possibly change in the next years to permit money remain on the market with no hyper-inflation risk?

Inflation targets are unrealistic as well. It is useless to say that in the latest years inflation targets of 25–30% were decided but all those years ended with huge inflations.

Unemployment targets are not more realistic either. The scenario envisages a serious drop in unemployment.

However, there are only two possibilities: either it drops but the Romanian economy will not be restructured or it will remain high and the economy will be able to restructure. The process will be longer than the fiver years the scenario allots to it.

Although the Strategy has restructuring as its main priority, it seems that the authors start from the premises that Romanian economy has already been restructured and will enter a period of development. The scenario has in view a more than 60% export increase in 2004 versus the achievements in 1999: from $8.5 billion to $13.6 billion. The achievements in 2000 and 2001 seem to meet these projects. However, the durability of the increase tendency cannot be assessed since there is no significant Romanian presence in other exports than the traditional ones: wood, footwear, or ready-made clothes.

On a whole, there is no doubt that substantial decrease in inflation, equally substantial decrease in unemployment, and significant increase in real wage for the following years are not possible.

These three targets could be reached if the supposed economic increase were accompanied by massive infusion of foreign resources. Unfortunately, this is not the case since the important foreign resources are not higher than 4–4.5% GDP equivalent.

Romania can only become credible if it makes up strategic scenarios that should show what its economy could do and not what it would like to do in the forthcoming five years.

44.3. Towards everything means towards nothing

The sector priorities are the great absence in the Strategy. Which sectors in Romanian economy could have real chances and prospects within the international competition? What could be done to protect them? Their absence is rather strange since a strategy means first to prioritize and then to direct the existing resources towards priorities. Several studies show that that Romanian economy has not many competitive advantages, except for its cheap workforce, and that would prioritize the internationally outdated and badly-paid sectors.

There Is a contradiction in Romania between the scarcity of resources and their waste in the absence of prioritizing that could direct them to sectors and activities with market chances and prospects. Prioritizing is not simple but in Romania it proves to be extremely complicated. After 12 years of groping for ways to save, with no money, the whole industry, it is almost impossible to find what sectors and activities the resources should be directed to. More than that, there is a risk in Romania that the resources could be prioritized according to political interests.

Generally speaking, the international financial institutions reject the idea of industrial politics based on sector priorities. However, the World Bank, forced to offer money for development, is more flexible than IMF that believes that it is for the market to decide the sectors orientation. However, neither IMF nor the World Bank takes two things into account.

The former is that all the present developed countries are the products of some industrial sector politics that helped them develop at least at the beginning. The international financial institutions pretend that that is history and happened at the beginning of the 1950s. Now, in the epoch of globalization and liberalizations, when economic success is conditioned by the observance of the market options, the developed countries abandoned the industrial sector politics and adopted the neutrality of public finances. However, they forget that Romania's situation is similar to that in the 1950s and that it can only hope to develop if its resources are focused to certain sectors.

The latter: the market can chose the best sectors and activities but this is the best option only when something is created on an empty place. Otherwise, major political decisions must be taken, with the observance of the market spirit of course, to get rid of the inefficient organizations and to support the efficient ones.

The Romanian case is highly significant. The international financial institutions prescribed for Romania a sector neutrality of public finance. In these conditions the market could not project any competitive activity in general and internationally competitive in particular. On the contrary, the Romanian economy is increasingly inefficient. The invisible hand of the market interrupted neither the inefficient inertial allocations nor the ones got by cliental criteria.
Although the IMF and World Bank recipes are mutually conditioned they are more often than not individualized by shades and differences. Anyhow they are not congruent with those coming from the European Union that has asked a sector-like approach of Romania. In fact the whole European Union construction lies on clear sector priorities, which change in time, as imposed by the world competition. Starting with the 1996s, here you are some famous examples: coal, steel, car industry, infrastructure, plane building, scientific research, informatics, and agriculture in the latest 40 years.

The European Union should coordinate its messages with those of IMF and of the World Bank. The varied signals coming from the above institutions have generated the worst thing of all: a continuous and disastrous improvisation.

As the integration negotiations go on, the messages and demands coming from the European Union (which has a market economy based on the strong corrective intervention of public politics) will gradually distance themselves from those coming from IMF and the World Bank (which support a market economy with so-called "neutral" public politics).

Romania needs quite a different type program than that applied until now: the essence of such a program is to refloat its investments. If the invisible hand of the market could not achieve it, refloating has to be promoted by public politics.

44.4. Neither less nor more, but better

The only counterargument is that the State has proved to be a bad investor and the money got for investments could be directed to bankrupt projects, to unproductive organizations, or to the governing political forces and their economic supporters. However a clear and restrictive legal framework could limit such abuses or at least part of them.

The invisible hand of the market could be more efficient but for 11–12 years it did nothing in Romania. Without investments Romanian economy will go for the worse.

The international context generated by the terrorist attacks on the United States inevitable influences Romania as well. The possible higher oil price, the dollar devaluation if recession persists in American economy and mainly a restriction of the export markets following reduction of the world economic activity would influence directly the Romanian economy. Likewise, one should consider the indirect effects generated by a general lack of confidence: from the investors' reticence to the increase in the price of credits. However, the deepest effects will be generated by the political and military consequences within international relations. These effects are medium- and long-term because the respective consequences are still looming.

The dispute over the role of the State in economy could be reopened. Following the tragic events in September 11, 2001 which changed the Americans' behavior towards consumption, the United States suddenly remembered Keynes and his recipes: interest reductions, selective fiscal facilities, support, and even subsidies.

Several decades ago, Keynes' theories had been abandoned in favor of some other approaches – massive lack of involvement of the State, an economy completely opened to abroad, strict currency control, etc. – perfectly justified for the western countries in the given context. The new approach was beneficial because it helped western countries reach balance, consolidate their prosperity, and get non-inflationist economic growth.

Unfortunately, the West asked the other countries of the world to give up Keynes as well although those countries had quite different development stages. Now, decades after the generalization of the economic recipes prescribed by the West the world has become even more polarized than it used to be: the globalization fruit is concentrated in few countries only whereas international frustrations are increasingly dramatic.

Within this unbearable and exasperating polarization, international terrorism can find both the best ground and motivations (confuse, but indestructible).

If the West, through IMF and the World Bank, does not amend the recipes it imposed on the underdeveloped countries that "dilated" the polarization, it will have to face more and more violent contestation. Those living in prosperity can be pacifist because they have all the reasons to be so. The poor can become violent any time because they have nothing to lose. And because they have nothing to lose they cannot be defeated.

In these conditions the IMF and the World Bank recipes will probably be amended and the State involvement in economy will be increasingly significant.

However, the case of Romania is different since the State is too much involved in economy. Therefore the issue of the State role in the Romanian economy is that of the quality of public politics: it should be neither less nor more, but better.

CHAPTER 45

Between "colonization" and "dictatorship"

I do not know Mr. Adrian Nastase's present opinions, when his party has taken over the helm, but in 1996 he tried to stigmatize the result of the then administration describing Romania to be somewhere "between colonization and dictatorship".

The wording "between colonization and dictatorship" dramatically describes all the menaces. Romania runs the risk of becoming a colony in the conditions of: economic underdevelopment, lack of industrialization, unprepared and uncompetitive economy that has to face the aggressive international competition. Likewise it can become a dictatorship: if the political class does not promote "heroic" solutions to break the present logjam, the parliamentary democracy is no longer able to face the massive social convulsions generated by atrophy of economic life.

Now then, there are two aspects. The former: is it realistic to think that a foreign partner would want to take the Romanian economy as a whole, with assets and liabilities? The international experience offers some good examples. Eastern Germany was taken over by West Germany but, of course, that was an exception. However, partial takeovers took place in: Hungary, Czech Republic, or Poland. Of course, the contribution of the political class in those countries cannot be ignored. The Romanian political parties would probably react in a different way to a possible "takeover" but they should not worry: Romania is in no danger of being "bought" or taken over by anybody!

The latter: could an iron-fist government be the solution? A dictatorship would have a lot of work to do in the present Romania: from putting a stop to the State dissolution to economic recovery. The problem an iron-fist government has to face would be an international acceptance of such a regime. However, such a regime should be both wise and skillful to properly implement its power.

The results of the general elections at the end of 2000 did not change the fundamental data: Romania is still *between.*

The most probable variant is that Romania will go the same way. It is on that way that a new element emerged somewhat unexpectedly: the Helsinki decision of the European Union to invite Romania to negotiations.

Without ignoring the historic significance of the invitation, the interpretation of some of the Romanian politicians that following such an act Romania's dramatic problems will disappear cannot be agreed with.

However, the Helsinki decision does not remove the big unknowns in the "between colonization and dictatorship" equation. There is no doubt that a candidate country to the European Union cannot become a dictatorship. On the other hand, European Union does not seem to have the slightest intention to change Romania into a colony. Unfortunately, the European Union seems disinclined to spend too much on Romania or for Romania, although Romania costs very little: about several billion dollars. But its problems are serious and they cost billions of dollars yearly for many decades from now on. There is one more question left: will the change supposed by a possible involvement of the European Union be strong enough to shatter the Romanian political class fossilized as it is in party, clan, and private interests?

By the same author:

Transnational corporations (1978)

Energy: imperative reconsiderations (1981)

Terra: a black-and-white portrait (about world resources, 1984)

Debt of the developing countries (1987)

Reform in Romania. Half measures double social costs (1994)

Manifest of the Immobilist Party (1996)

Politicians, businesspeople (in the volume *Romania* 1986–1999, *The struggle with ourselves*, 1999)

Can the vicious circle be broken? (in the volume *Economic transition in Romania. Past, present, and future*, 2000)